TURNED BOXES
50 designs

TURNED BOXES
50 designs

Chris Stott

Guild of Master Craftsman Publications Ltd

First published 2002 by
Guild of Master Craftsman Publications Ltd
Castle Place, 166 High Street
Lewes, East Sussex BN7 1XU

Reprinted 2002, 2003

Edited by Stephen Haynes
Designed by Fineline Studios
Cover design by Lovelock & Co
Set in Myriad

Colour origination by Viscan Graphics (Singapore)
Printed and bound in Hong Kong by CT Printing Ltd

Dedicated to

My father-in-law, the late Mr Fred Turner, who sadly died during the writing of this book.

Acknowledgements

I thank Alan Neal for his work in drawing all the plans, and my wife, family and friends for their support and help in getting established as a woodturner, and for helping to produce this book.

I would also very much like to thank Allan Batty, Michael Hosaluk, Ray Key, Kip Christensen and Hans Joachim Weissflog for agreeing to provide photographs for the Gallery selection. These are five of my favourite woodturners, who have taken box making to new heights.

The following manufacturers and suppliers have been particularly helpful in providing information about their products: Craft Supplies Ltd, Millers Dale, Derbyshire (timber, machinery, tools and accessories); Poolewood Machinery, Sittingbourne, Kent (machinery, tools and accessories); Robert Sorby Ltd, Sheffield (tools); Henry Taylor (Tools) Ltd, Sheffield (tools); Timberline, Tonbridge, Kent (exotic timbers); GPS Agencies, Chichester, West Sussex (alternative ivory and similar materials); Craft Supplies, Provo, Utah, USA (machinery, tools, accessories and timber); Packard Woodworks, Tryon, North Carolina, USA (machinery and tools).

Measurements

Although care has been taken to ensure that the imperial measurements are true and accurate, they are only conversions from metric. When following the projects, use either the metric or the imperial measurements; do not mix units.

Photocopying

The working drawings in this book have been printed with generous margins so that readers may easily photocopy them to the required size for their own private use; but please note that they may not be reproduced commercially without the permission of the designer and copyright owner.

Photographic credits

Photographs are by Anthony Bailey, © GMC Publications Ltd 2002, with the following exceptions: those on pages 11, 12, 13, 16, 20, 21, 31, 36 (bottom), 41, 42, 43, 48, 50–1, 64 (bottom), 66–7, 175 are by the author; those in the Gallery were kindly supplied by the turners concerned.

Contents

Foreword

I have known Chris Stott for many years, and he has well earned his reputation as one of Britain's most respected, accomplished and successful woodturners.

After many years honing his skills and attaining an exceedingly high degree of technical ability, he has also gained worldwide recognition for his innovative and exciting woodturning creations. He is equally adept at producing all types of exquisite turnings, from small boxes to large bowls, platters and hollow forms. Accordingly, he is in great demand as a teacher and demonstrator, both in Britain and overseas.

First impressions of Chris can be misleading, and some might think he is rather dour and humourless. However, one has only to sit in on one of his demonstrations to realize that he has an exceptional, dry sense of humour. More importantly, he has the ability to communicate to his audience the enlightening and interesting points without recourse to unnecessary verbiage.

Chris's videos on all aspects of woodturning have been acclaimed by many as some of the best available. He has also occasionally committed himself to the written word in articles for the various woodworking magazines. Therefore it came as no surprise to me when he finally got round to publishing a book.

And what a good one it is too! Describing the making of 50 different designs of boxes is a daunting task, but Chris has made the book eminently readable by keeping repetition and cross-referencing to the minimum.

I am also very impressed by Alan Neal's line drawings. In addition to being produced to a high standard, it is refreshing to see that almost all of them have been drawn full size, which is of great benefit to the less experienced turner.

The designs of the boxes are sensibly arranged in ascending order of difficulty. The early ones require only basic equipment and can be completed in one fixing, without recourse to reverse-chucking or 'jam-fit' techniques. Later designs demand more sophisticated methods.

It would be fatuous to expect everyone to admire all the designs, but it is safe to say that there is something for every taste. Sensible and constructive advice is also given on safety measures, tool requirements and sharpening, and – this is of vital importance – the inherent pitfalls involved in box making and how to avoid them.

The author's intention in writing the book was to provide some inspiration to the less experienced turner who relishes the challenge of box turning. It will certainly do that, but many a seasoned professional could also learn a great deal.

Some would argue that the skill required to produce a reasonable box is beyond the substantial number of turners at the bottom end of the learning curve. I don't agree. Any type of turning requires a high level of skill if a pleasing end product is to be attained, and some of the boxes in this book are well within the range of the turner possessing only modest skills.

Accordingly, I feel that this book will appeal to all levels, and I am of the opinion that no woodturner's library should be without a copy.

Keith Rowley
Nottingham, England, 2001

Introduction

The purpose of this book is not to provide designs for commercial woodturners to market, but to give some level of inspiration to the less experienced turner who would like the challenge of turning boxes. The designs start with the simplest concept of a turned box, and develop into more complicated and involved projects. Although there are only 50 actual plans, there are so many woods available, and so many possible variations in design, that if you are so inclined, you may never turn two boxes alike.

Some of the designs, such as the Apple or Mushroom boxes, have been inspired by natural objects. A few have been 'borrowed' from other turners. Where I am aware of this, I have credited the original maker in the text. However, over the years I have seen so many pieces, made by such a multitude of turners, that I may sometimes have been influenced without knowing it. If you feel I have used a design that is yours and not mentioned your name, please accept my apologies. Sometimes a notion comes into my head and I have no idea where it originated.

When learning a new craft, it is the most natural thing in the world to copy existing items, and in my opinion there is nothing wrong in this. Artists have copied old masters for generations in order to understand their techniques. Eventually, though, there comes a time when you have to put something of yourself into your work and develop a style that is unique to you. I hope these designs will help to get you started on this path.

Part I
Technique and Inspiration

The products made by this pole-lathe turner include water flasks of the kind which inspired my Flask boxes (no. 50 and below). The woodcut is from Jost Amman and Hans Sachs, *The Book of Trades* (*Ständebuch*), first published in Nuremberg in 1568 (by courtesy of Dover Publications, Inc.)

A variation on the Flask box (no. 50) in Osage orange and violet rosewood
h. 115mm (4^{17}/$_{32}$in), d. 78mm (3^{5}/$_{64}$in)

A brief history of turned boxes

It appears that the woodturners of today belong to a craft with a very long history. Although items which look turned have been found in the pyramids of ancient Egypt, no evidence of the lathe has so far been found in the sculptures – whereas the potter and his wheel, along with various other trades, are plainly depicted. Fortunately there is documented evidence that the early Greeks and Romans were quite familiar with the turning process, so it is quite possible that the lathe was one of the first machine tools ever developed.

Recently the remains of an ancient woodturning centre were discovered in York, England. However, wood being as it is, most of the details have rotted away and only sparse evidence survives. It is not possible to say whether they were making boxes as well as the bowls and platters for which there is definite evidence.

These days we all accept pills in plastic containers, ointments in plastic or pressed metal boxes, and cosmetics in cardboard or other packaging. For several hundred years before these materials were available, the natural choice was a wooden container, and these were familiar items in the home or workplace. These small turned wooden artefacts are collectively known as *treen*. The Pinto Collection, housed in the Birmingham (England) Museum and Art Gallery, must be the greatest collection of these items in the world. There are over 6,000 pieces in the museum, many of which are displayed in the Pinto Gallery itself.

When I visited the Pinto Gallery my personal interest was, not surprisingly, boxes and containers. It was amazing to see mundane articles such as matchboxes, snuffboxes, containers for cosmetics and patent remedies, all crafted from wood. Of course, there were varying levels of quality: a gentleman's snuffbox, finely decorated and with a threaded lid, required far more time and skill than the humble box for matches. One real surprise was a pair of travelling candlesticks that screwed together, the bases of which fitted together as a box and contained the stems and candle snuffers – just what every travelling gentleman needed.

Another item that caught my eye was a compact drinking set, the base of which was a container for the liquor. Into this screwed a tumbler, and the top was a box to hold herbs with which the brew could be spiced. Every piece was turned from wood, and when fitted together they formed the shape of a bottle. A set of stacked herb containers was also impressive, each box forming the lid for the one below. I wonder how many of us would attempt this, even with our modern machinery.

Most of the everyday articles would have been turned on a pole lathe, which has no chuck and can only hold the work between centres, leaving a small piece of waste wood in the centre to be carved away. The marks where this was done can often be seen on the finished article. Hollowing was probably accomplished using a hook tool made by the local blacksmith.

It is interesting to note that designs were often copied from the vessels made by the silversmiths of the period, and, as silver articles carry a dated hallmark, reasonably accurate dates can be attributed to the wooden equivalents.

Nothing much changes: we modern turners adapt designs from ceramics and other materials for our craft. Although articles of wood have never reached the status of ceramics or glass, in terms of perceived value, some turners are now making inroads into this undervaluing of our craft.

In earlier ages customers did not need to travel; all needs could be accommodated by local craftsmen. Even in my youth, I remember being introduced to someone who had never been more than three miles from her home in a remote rural village. Craftsmen, however, did travel a little more than most, as they were expected to work for a variety of masters during the journeyman stage of their training, after apprenticeship. In this way knowledge and skills were shared and spread between areas.

In 1539 Holbein painted a miniature portrait of Anne of Cleves which was presented to Henry VIII in an exquisite engine-turned ivory case, decorated with a stylized Tudor rose. This and other ivory boxes are in the miniature collection at the Victoria and Albert Museum, London. These beautiful examples of the ornamental turner's art have survived for over four and a half centuries. Though pieces of this kind are well outside the scope of this book, it amazes me that the machinery and the skill needed to make articles such as these were perfected so long ago. Apparently there was a turner attached to the court of King Henry who was responsible for these works of art.

Somewhat later, with the opening up of trade with the New World, lignum vitae and other dense exotic woods became available, and there are many more boxes, vessels and lidded cups made in these timbers, which survive in collections.

I have never turned ivory but, from reading, I know it to be a homogeneous material with few, if any, faults, which makes it well suited to work of this nature. By contrast, the use of wood, as we all know, brings the problems of cracking during seasoning, warping, and inherent faults in the timber. The old craftsmen must have gone through the process of rough-turning the items and then drying the wood over a long period before the final turning – otherwise the work would not have survived in its present state. Even so, maybe, it is mainly the items from the grand country houses that have survived, while the millions of mundane articles from the lower orders have over the years provided fodder for the fire.

Nowadays boxes can be mass-produced on an automatic lathe and churned out by the thousands at a low price. However, the quality is usually low and the finish leaves much to be desired. There are also many imports from the Third World which are sold in craft or gift shops at prices below that at which we in the West can purchase the wood. Once again the quality is often pretty low and the finish treacly. I have seen some boxes from India which were cleverly inlaid with brass and had a certain amount of appeal, but even these lacked something in design and finish.

On this note, I have to say that my visits to craft fairs as a potential customer have been very disappointing. Looking at the quality of some turnings on sale makes me wonder when the average hobbyist will learn that a quality product will sell, and that putting poorly made items on display only degrades the image of woodturning.

After years of mass production, many customers are again prepared to pay a little more in order to get handcrafted one-off boxes which have had care lavished on the finish and thought given to the design process. America is perhaps further along this road than the UK. Britain has such a long history of utilitarian articles being made of wood that we still have a long way to go before the general public appreciates that a wooden article can also be an artistic one, and that craftsmanship is worth paying for.

A woodturner's life

The following account is not intended as an ego trip, but to show the way in which external forces influenced my concept of how boxes should be made for various markets. Above all, it illustrates the process by which I learnt what the customer wanted, and came to understand that if the starter woodturner wants to eat he must pay attention to what customers tell him. Later on, as you will see, the luxury of doing one's own thing becomes a possibility.

Boxes have always been a popular project for woodturners, partly because they demand a fairly high degree of skill, but also because they usually seem to sell reasonably well. One reason for their being a marketable item is that they are perceived as being 'useful' as well as decorative. Many people can be persuaded to buy an item they can use, whereas, in England at least, fewer will purchase a wooden item that they see as merely decorative.

Even before I started turning professionally, I visited craft fairs to try and assess what products were the most likely to sell. I saw some very poor woodturning: tooling rings in the bottom of bowls were described as the trademark of a hand-turned item, a dead matt surface as an oiled finish, and green baize on the underside of pieces covered a multitude of sins. But then I came across a turner who had small vases in his display: beautiful classical shapes turned from exotic woods, and superbly finished with a high shine. I do not know who he was, but his attention to detail left a permanent impression on me. I wanted to turn these fabulous woods, with their striking colours and grain patterns – though I felt that the vases themselves had a very limited market.

Inset-lid box (see no. 37) in ebony and cocobolo
h. 76mm (3in), d. 56mm (2³/₁₆in)

When turning for the craft fairs, I did make vases in simple shapes, for dried flowers and grasses, and called them 'weed pots'. Frequently they were turned from yew branch wood or spalted beech. The exotic woods were reserved for boxes, and, as most of the shows were held under canvas in rather poor light conditions, the brightest-coloured woods were selected: padauk, purpleheart and hornbeam, along with the superb grain of cocobolo and the ultimate contrast of ebony. My early attempts at producing saleable boxes would win no prizes today as far as design is

Ugly round-edged box in zebrano: sometimes the grain can overpower the design

Underside of the same box, showing incised rings h. 50mm (1^{31}/$_{32}$in), d. 93mm (3^{21}/$_{32}$in)

concerned. They were undoubtedly boxes, as they had lids that covered the opening, but I still cringe when people say they have a box bought from me in the early years. I do keep some boxes from these early days, as a reminder of where it all started. Not worthy of being put on show, they can only be described as ugly. They do, however, help students to see that things can get better: as control of the tools develops, the eye becomes more critical, and the shapes improve.

In the early 1980s there were only two magazines on the subject of woodwork, and they covered the whole spectrum, from cabinetmaking to carving, so woodturning had minimal coverage. Most present-day turners would not even recognize the names of the people who wrote the articles. Hence, there was very little to inspire a budding turner. Woodturning was still a solitary hobby, individual turners doing their own thing in their garden shed or garage, and having no contact with other turners – unless they met at a craft fair, where they were competitors, and each jealously guarded their own secrets on technique and finishing materials.

Dale Nish's two books, *Creative Woodturning* (1975) and *Artistic Woodturning* (1980; both published by Brigham Young University Press, Provo, Utah), had a profound effect on my own efforts. Here was someone who gave detailed instruction on many aspects of the craft, with pages of step-by-step photographs on each project. There was information on harvesting the timber, and how to convert it into useful items by first rough-turning, then allowing it to dry and stabilize. Many of the projects utilized simple techniques that transformed the mundane into the artistic. One aspect that particularly appealed to me was that the projects in these books used no ready-made fittings. Most of the turners on the craft-fair circuit had clocks, barometers and teapot stands on display; I had already made the decision to have only wood on my stand, and not to be a retailer for the companies selling these accessories. Hence, these books gave both instruction and inspiration to me – and, I suspect, a great many other turners as well. I do feel that Dale's books played an important part in the great upsurge of interest in our craft that occurred in the 1980s. I never dreamed then that one day I would not only meet Dale and work alongside him as a presenter at an international seminar, but actually stay at his home in Provo, Utah.

Turning boxes professionally: the craft-fair circuit

In the beginning I started selling my work by attending local one-day fairs. These were run by two enthusiastic woodworkers and took place in village halls in the north of England. A table cost £8 for the day, but often I was asked to fill more than one table due to a poor take-up by the other craft workers, and I sometimes had 15ft of space for my modest fee. Advertising was minimal and amounted to a few lines in the local papers. The visitors were sometimes few and far between, but it was a good way to find out what people wanted to buy and how much they were prepared to pay for it.

I had been excited by a photograph of a natural-edged bowl in one of Dale Nish's books, so I always had several burr elm ones on show, along with the weed pots and ugly boxes. 'Are they coconuts?' 'What were they before they broke?' were some of the comments I heard, but fortunately there were also visitors with a little taste who appreciated the appeal of something different. In those days natural-edged bowls were virtually unknown in Britain outside the world of competitions and exhibitions. Unknown to me, turners in America had been making them since the 1940s, but as I said earlier there was very little communication between turners in Britain, let alone between Britain and the USA. It was many years later that I learned that the British turners Richard Raffan and Ray Key had been demonstrating in America in the early 1980s, before I had even started woodturning.

Somewhere along the line you have to put your work alongside that of your peers, and see how you measure up. With this in mind I answered an advert and booked a table in the Craft area of the *Practical Woodworker* Exhibition at the

Pill box (see no. 13) in ebony and pink ivory
h. 33mm (1⁵⁄₁₆in), d. 44mm (1³⁄₄in)

Wembley Conference Centre for the four days of the show. Tables could be booked by the day, and once again I was asked if I could fill additional tables at no extra cost, as very few people had booked for the Thursday and Friday. We had a ball! My wife and I were busy, selling and packing. It was the best response we had ever experienced. Other craft-fair turners could not understand why I had booked this venue, as they thought it impossible to sell to other woodturners – but we did, and to many other people as well. What they did not appreciate was that not only turners go to such shows. Cabinetmakers, toy makers, joiners, in fact any person with a love of wood can be seen at these events – hence our success. By lunchtime on the Saturday we were struggling to fill half a table, and we were allowed to pack up and leave late on the Sunday morning, having sold everything except for a few bowls.

There were a few well-known turners at the show, demonstrating on the trade stands. Just two of them stopped to talk: Phil Reardon and Allan Batty. Allan's comment 'I like your work – keep it up' was all the encouragement I needed, and I thank him for taking the trouble to stop and look. Ever since then I have tried to work on the basis that an ounce of encouragement is worth a pound of criticism, and if you have to criticize it should be constructive. This is a stark contrast to the comments I overheard outside a craft fair in a northern resort. Two old ladies were chatting and one of them said 'We'll not go in there – it's only things they've made themselves.'

With this measure of success I started booking stands at larger shows. As the income grew I bought a van and a caravan (trailer). It was sheer luxury to be able to carry a lathe and as much stock as needed, and to have a hot shower in the caravan after a long day behind the stand. The downside was that water had to be hauled from a tap somewhere in an invariably muddy field.

Many of the shows we booked were with the Rural Crafts Association. This organization booked space for large marquees at all the major agricultural, county and flower shows, as well as equestrian events like the Burghley Horse Trials.

Initially the number of shows we were allowed to book was limited, but as we proved successful and showed that we did not run out of stock, we were allowed into the bigger and better venues.

The show year started in early May and went on into September. Often one event followed another and we were away from home for days. The longest time away that I remember was 21 days, during which we attended four shows: Hertfordshire, Surrey, Bath and West, finishing up at the South of England Show at Ardingly in West Sussex. Time dulls the memory and the numbers do not seem to add up now, so maybe there was another show along the way. We got to the stage where someone would say 'We are at the Royal Show, so it must be July.' Time means little when every spare day is spent in the workshop.

Our life continued like this for several years, frantically making stock throughout the winter and leading an almost nomadic existence selling my work during the summer. At least, it was technically summer, but the large number of

Square-sided box in satinwood with chattered ebony insert
h. 40mm (1^{19}/$_{32}$in), d. 46mm (1^{13}/$_{16}$in)

shows where it rained, and the public trudged around in mud, stick in my mind.

When the weather is hot the people don't come into the marquees, and when it is wet they drip over your display, or stay away altogether. You are always at the mercy of the organizer, or the weather, or both. On top of all that, you are committed to making the items you know will sell. It is very difficult to find the time to experiment.

The basic catch-22 is that if you want to sell you have to attend more shows, which leaves less time to make your products. One answer might be to let someone else sell the work. This is fine, as it leaves you in the workshop making the goods and shipping them out to galleries or craft shops. However, you then have to sell at half the price because the gallery needs to put on a mark-up – often 100%, plus tax. I do not begrudge this, because the cost of keeping a gallery has to be met. What I did not like was losing the contact with the general public. Hence I never actively sought contacts with galleries.

Over the years several galleries have approached me and bought a selection of my work. Some have come back with repeat orders, others have had no further contact. I suspect what happens is that when work goes on display, local turners move in and say 'I make pieces like these.' Having work brought to your gallery in this way is obviously easier than ordering by post or phone, and far better than travelling miles to make a selection, so they buy from the local turner instead.

For these reasons I have never tried to promote myself to the trade, and never applied to exhibit at a trade show, even though I do now turn pieces that I could call, for want of a better name, 'gallery items'. I would rather do a one-off exhibition, or stick to the small boxes that I can take with me on my travels. I still sell some items through a superb gallery that specializes in wood, but they approached me many years ago and we now seem to have a special relationship. The owner rings up each year and I send a selection – long may it continue!

Round-edged box in violet rosewood
h. 39mm (1^{17}/$_{32}$in), d. 45mm (1^{25}/$_{32}$in)

Later years

Sometimes you get a lucky break. Mine happened one year as we were preparing to set off on one of our multi-venue trips. The organizer rang me to say that Badminton Horse Trials had been cancelled due to a cloudburst and there was no way that the ground would dry out in time for the horses to compete. This meant that we would have a five-day gap in the middle of the trip. Because I had been seen at many shows, several other organizers sent me details of their events. One of these was the *Woodworker* exhibition at Bristol, the dates for which fitted perfectly with the cancelled dates for Badminton. I rang the organizer to ask if there was any space left, and we were in. There was a Caravan Club site close by the old docks in the centre of the town, so our problem was solved.

On arrival we set up as usual, and on the first day a man came and bought some pieces, introducing himself as the assistant editor of *Woodworker* magazine. He returned later with the editor, and once again with two young ladies who were introduced as the company's show organizers. They asked if I would exhibit at the Alexandra Palace *Woodworker* Show and be the demonstrator for the magazine. Of course I would! With a free stand in the middle of the show, my name in the magazine and a new status as an expert woodturner, who wouldn't?

There were other benefits as well. A representative from one of the major tool manufacturers came to the stand and was horrified by the state of the tools I was using. Many of them were 'seconds', bought from a local market stall. 'Come with me, take what you need,' he said, standing in front of their full range of turning tools.

I had started a long relationship with the magazine, demonstrating for them at Alexandra Palace and later at Sandown Park when the venue was changed. This continued until the magazine was taken over by another publishing house, and the character of the show seemed to change. By this time I was demonstrating for a lathe manufacturer, I had written several articles for magazines, and established my name in the turning world.

International demonstrations

My first trip abroad was at the request of Craft Supplies (UK), who had donated a Stewart system as a prize to the Irish Woodturners' Seminar held in Sligo. (This is a system, designed by the American turner Dennis Stewart, primarily for hollowing vessels through a small opening. All the components, mostly with scraping tips, fit into an arm-brace handle, giving excellent control over each operation.) I was to take the tool over there and demonstrate its use between the presentations. Later, I was invited to Sweden and to the first ever seminar in Germany. Former students invited me to Guernsey in the Channel Isles, and another to Iceland, on teaching trips. A weekend demonstrating at open days at Stavanger in Norway led to my being included, along with two other British turners, on a boat trip through the Norwegian fjords, demonstrating at each stop.

I have also been involved in English seminars which have allowed me to meet several of the leading American turners such as John Jordan and David Ellsworth. The former helped me a great deal on my first visit to America by organizing several demos. Since that first trip to the USA in 1994 I have returned each year, and, as well as workshops and demonstrations, I have been a presenter at three international conferences.

Woodturning has been very good to me over the years: I have made a lot of friends and enjoyed meeting all the 'wood nuts'.

Safety in the workshop

The woodturning lathe should be the safest of all woodworking machines, since it does not have rotating metal cutters – all it does is spin wood. In my experience, all accidents attributed to the wood lathe are caused by silly mistakes on the part of the operator. We can all have lapses in concentration which result in a 'dig-in', but these should not be so drastic as to tear the wood from the lathe. However, there are times when other factors accumulate, such as the chuck not being tight enough, or the lathe centres not biting deeply enough into the wood, and this is when accidents happen.

Cutting

For safety, always approach the cut in a firm yet deliberate manner, with the bevel of the tool rubbing on the wood, and, to minimize any risks, increase the depth of cut by lifting the handle of the gouge rather than pushing into the work.

Lathe height

The height of the lathe is quite critical for the turner's welfare. Measure the distance from elbow to floor with your arm bent: this gives you the ideal centre height for the lathe for general turning. If you only turn small items, such as boxes, then having it a little higher is an advantage, as you often need to inspect the inside, and the less you have to bend your back, the better. Above all, you have to feel comfortable whilst working. If I demonstrate on a lathe that is only a couple of inches too low I can be sure of backache the next day.

Clothing and hair

Loose clothing, especially sleeves, should always be avoided, long hair needs to be tied back and preferably enclosed by a cap, and even fingernails can be caught by the wood and torn. This can be quite painful and may stop you turning for a day or two, so keep them trimmed short.

Eye protection

Eyes should be protected at all times by wearing either a full face mask or goggles. The whole idea of woodturning is to remove shavings, and these can easily find their way to an unprotected eye.

The risk to eyes is even greater when grinding tools. Particles of metal from a 6in grinder can be travelling at almost 60mph as they leave the stone, and there is no time to blink, so always wear a face mask when using the grinder. Having good light on the grinder is also a very good idea, especially as middle age comes on and eyesight deteriorates a little.

Dust

This is the most hazardous aspect of woodturning. We all have to sand, and this creates dust. Some woods are more hazardous than others; some are even carcinogenic or can cause allergy problems. One of the worst is spalted wood, because it is impregnated with mould spores which will really flourish in the damp, warm environment of your lungs.

It is obviously advisable to wear a dust mask and, as soon as it can be afforded, a dust extractor is invaluable. However, most of the extractors only take out the larger particles, and it is often the finest particles, almost invisible to the naked eye, which do most damage. There are also electrically powered respirator helmets available which do an excellent job of removing the very fine particles, though they can feel heavy and clumsy on the head and take some getting used to. On tricky woods I quite often use both the helmet and the extractor together.

Allergies

Speaking of tricky woods, I know turners who cannot work with woods like cocobolo because even the dust on their skin creates a painful rash. One friend of mine even had to retire early from work after yew dust exacerbated his asthma. The danger is that once you have become allergic to one species you become sensitized, and others can start affecting you. Woods that often seem to cause problems include cocobolo, spalted timbers, yew and Santos rosewood, but there are many, many more.

Rags

I do not allow these in the workshop at all. I used to use them for all sorts of jobs, until a friend of mine lost the end of his little finger just polishing a light-pull on the lathe. The rag was grabbed by the wood, lassoed his finger, and pulled the end section straight off at the joint. Since then I have only used kitchen paper (soft paper towels), even

for polishing. It works just as well as cloth, is more absorbent, and there is always a clean bit waiting on the roll to be used. A rag can pull your fingers into the work, but a paper towel will just tear away.

Solvents

Some woodturning finishes use solvents which can be regarded as hazardous; in fact, the European Community is trying to reduce the use of many of them. However, I feel that we use them in such small quantities that, as long as people are sensible, they should cause few problems. Smokers like myself, of course, have to be more careful than others.

Offcuts

Leaving these lying around on the floor has caused many a trip over the years; I now keep a big dustbin and try to use it. I do tend to leave shavings around under the lathe to act as a cushion for anything that I drop on the floor, but this does create a fire hazard and should be cleared up at the end of each day. Also, of course, it is a good way to lose small tools, which bury themselves and are hard to find. Some turners attach a bobbin to small items or put red paint on them to help with retrieval. I keep a magnet on the headstock to retain Allen keys and callipers.

Bandsaws

These are a significant health hazard, both with dust and the danger to fingers. I know many turners who have been far too flippant when using a bandsaw and suffered as a result. When acquiring one of these it is probably as well to follow the safety recommendations made by the manufacturers.

The general message about safety is: 'Think safe and be safe.'

Tools and machinery

A box can be turned on any lathe, so whatever machine you have, as long as it will spin a piece of wood without vibration, you should have few problems in that department.

Lathes

My first lathe was a Union Jubilee, the forerunner of the Graduate, welded up from steel plate rather than being made from cast iron. In those days I made only simple boxes for craft fairs, and the lathe was set to run at full speed (2,250rpm) through the whole process of my box making. Now I make more complicated designs, and require more control of the speed. All three of my present lathes are fitted with electronic control, allowing me to vary the speed at the turn of a dial.

The first is a Poolewood Euro 2000, a superb lathe, bench-mounted, very heavy and extremely powerful. Although I used this on my video *Inlaid and Novelty Boxes*, it would not be my first choice now, as it is not so user-friendly for the quite intricate process of box making. The toolrest is big and heavy, as is the tailstock – which is just what is needed for the larger project, but they feel rather clumsy when making smaller items.

My second lathe is a Poolewood Euro 1000, which is also a bench-mounted machine, and bought as a replacement for the 28/40 that I used for eight years. This lathe is much more suited to turning small-scale items such as boxes: the toolrest is quick to position, the speed is infinitely variable, and the direct drive results in a very smooth and quiet machine. Even though the 1000 is a smaller machine

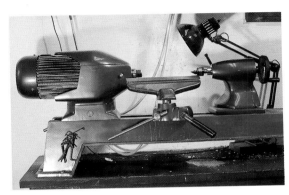

My Poolewood Euro 2000 lathe

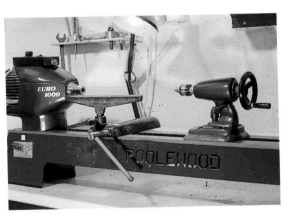

Poolewood Euro 1000

than its big brother, the bench I have mounted it on is just as heavy and solid. For the top I used a length of kitchen worktop 600mm (24in) wide and 30mm (1¼in) thick. Being covered with laminate, it is easily wiped clean, although most of the time it is covered in shavings and tools. An advantage of having such a wide top to the bench is that I can have it butting up to the workshop wall, so no tools are lost down the back. If I ever found it necessary, I could fix brackets between the worktop and the wall, giving extra support to the whole bench.

Woodfast short-bed lathe

The Craft Supplies Precision Collet Chuck on the Woodfast lathe

The third lathe in the shop is an Australian short-bed Woodfast; this is the machine I dismantle and transport to demonstrations. Originally it had a 1hp, four-speed pulley drive, but I have had it converted to electronic speed control and fitted a 1.5hp motor. With its cast-iron bed and very solid construction it is another excellent lathe, and it is not surprising that it is one of the most popular machines sold in America. One limitation is that the base cabinet is rather narrow, but this is not much of a disadvantage when turning small items. It can be a problem when turning items 400mm (16in) in diameter, but I have combated this by fitting feet that extend out from the back, giving it much more stability. All three lathes are set with their centre height at 1220mm (48in).

Chucks

It is possible to turn a box using only a screw chuck, but this would waste a great deal of wood. On the Continent the preference is for simple cup chucks; however, I think these put a lot of undue stress on the bearings as the wood is hammered into the chuck.

I use the following six chucks:

1 Ever since it was designed, I have used a Craft Supplies (UK) Precision Collet Chuck, which holds on a 38mm (1½in) spigot less than 3mm (⅛in) long. Its compact size, excellent grip and lack of sharp edges made it the ideal chuck for boxes. Sadly, it is no longer available, and the collets now fit into the larger-diameter Combination Chuck, which unfortunately restricts access to the base of the work.

2 My other chuck in general use is the Poolewood Compact Chuck. This will grip any spigot from 50mm (2in) to over 75mm (3in), which makes it very versatile.

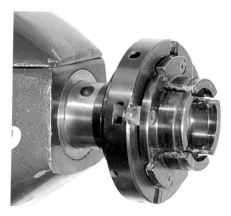

Poolewood Compact Chuck

The One-Way Stronghold Chuck on the Woodfast lathe

3 I have a One-Way Stronghold Chuck that fits only the Woodfast lathe. The shaped jaws of this chuck can grip square or round stock. I also have a set of collets to fit the Stronghold, and these will grip dowels from 13mm ($\frac{1}{2}$in) to 38mm (1$\frac{1}{2}$in); I use these for occasional projects.

4 For off-centre or eccentric turning, I have used the simplest of adjustable screw chucks, the RTF Variant adaptor. The screw is held in a slot by an Allen screw, and by moving the wood screw partway through the process I can create a box turned on more than one axis, all the axes being parallel to one another. However, I now find this accessory is no longer available, so I have switched to the Sorby eccentric chuck. This is a much more sophisticated accessory, capable of many other operations.

5 With the Multistar chuck fitted with the Gim-Ball accessory I can vary the angle of the axis, and this gives some interesting possibilities.

6 Small square or round sections can be gripped in my Axminster four-jaw chuck fitted with the engineering jaws.

The Variant adaptor mounted on the Stronghold chuck

The Robert Sorby eccentric chuck

The Gim-Ball accessory on the Multistar chuck

The Axminster four-jaw chuck with engineering jaws

My recommended set of gouges *(left to right)*: **32mm (1¼in) roughing gouge, 12mm (½in) 'Continental' gouge, 10mm (³⁄₈in) and 6mm (¼in) spindle gouges**

25mm (1in) and 13mm (½in) oval-section skew chisels

Chisels and gouges

The basic set of tools required for making boxes is much the same as for any spindle turning. However, these are the ones that I use and recommend:

- Roughing gouge   32mm (1¼in)
- Spindle gouges   10mm (³⁄₈in) and
                                       6mm (¼in)
- Skew chisels   25mm (1in) and
                                       13mm (½in)
- Parting tools   6mm (¼in), 3mm (¹⁄₈in)
                                       and Superthin

The Chris Stott Superthin parting tool, 1.5mm (¹⁄₁₆in) wide, is made to my own design and is widely available in Britain and the USA.

I would add to these a 12mm (½in) 'Continental' gouge ground straight across so it looks like a small roughing gouge, which is precisely what I use it for. (A 'Continental' spindle gouge is one which is forged to shape rather than machined from a round bar.)

Scrapers

Much of the work on the inside of boxes is done with scrapers; the profiles of these will vary depending on the shapes of your boxes. The selection of scrapers I use most frequently has developed over the years, and these five will cope with most of my designs:

6mm (¼in) and 3mm (¹⁄₈in) conventional parting tools and the Chris Stott Superthin

A close-up of the 6mm (¼in) square-ended scraper, showing how the left edge is relieved to give more clearance

A close-up of the undercut scraper, reground from a round-ended tool

- 6mm (¼in) square-ended, kept very sharp on the corners; this is not available commercially, and I ground it myself from another tool
- 13mm (½in) square-ended, left corner rounded, and the sharpness removed on the right corner
- 13mm (½in) round-ended
- 19mm (¾in) undercut scraper; I ground this myself from a round-ended tool, to give support whilst undercutting
- 25mm (1in) heavy french curve, for larger boxes

All of these are relieved on the left-hand side so that the lower corner does not foul inside small diameters. The top surfaces are polished on a diamond hone and the grinding marks on the cutting edge removed, also using a diamond hone. This means that none of these scrapers have a burr at the cutting edge. I find that this gives me much more control over the cutting action; they are also much less likely to 'grab', and I achieve a much finer finish straight from the tool. The reason is that if a tool is ground on an 80-grit wheel, the scratches on the tool will be reproduced on the wood. If, however, the edge is polished, the cut will be much cleaner and will require less sanding.

My recommended set of scrapers *(left to right)*: **6mm (¼in) square-ended, 13mm (½in) square-ended with left corner rounded, 13mm (½in) round-ended, 19mm (¾in) undercut, 25mm (1in) french curve**

The Robert Sorby grinding jig, shown with the adjustable table raised

The Sorby grinding jig with the swivelling tool holder ready for use

Sharpening

Even the best tools in the world become useless pieces of metal if you cannot sharpen them. Sharp tools are a primary requirement for all aspects of turning. When I started woodturning, there were no jigs available, so I had to learn how to sharpen tools 'freehand', using only the toolrest on the grinder for guidance. When the first jigs appeared on the market, I argued that if a jig was needed to present the tool to the grinder, we would also need a jig to present the tool to the wood, as the movements are basically the same.

Many years of teaching students have taught me that if there is a device available to make a job easier, then we should take advantage of it. In fact, I often joke during demonstrations that if someone markets a gadget that will do half my work, I will buy two of them! A sharpening jig may cost the same as two or three tools, but in the long run the benefit of being able to grind a perfect fingernail shape on a spindle gouge, every time, could save that amount of tool steel.

I know that when I was learning to sharpen tools I ground away a great deal of metal before they started cutting to my satisfaction.

The question we are now faced with is which jig to use. There are several on the market, and of course they all work. The jig I use is the one made by Robert Sorby. This has an adjustable table that can be set to any angle, and is therefore ideal for the grinding of scrapers and skew chisels. The swivelling tool holder will create a perfect fingernail shape to my preferred angle on any gouge, and all this comes at a reasonable price and without a pile of accessories.

As stated earlier, I polish the edges of all the scrapers, but I use the gouges straight from the grinder; I find that the slightly serrated edge, used with a slicing action, gives me the ideal cut.

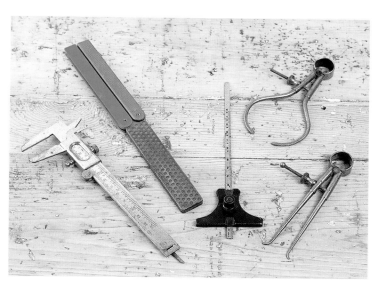

These are all essential tools for box making (*left to right*)**: vernier callipers, diamond hone, depth gauge, outside and inside callipers**

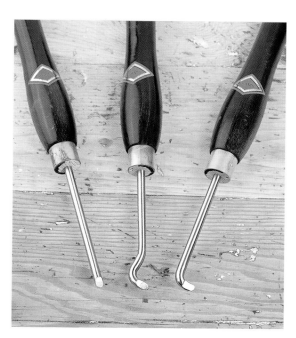

A set of Chris Stott Micro Hollowing Tools

Other equipment

Making small boxes requires a fair amount of precision, so you will need a selection of suitably sized measuring tools: vernier callipers, inside and outside callipers and a depth gauge.

The miniature hollow-form tools made by Henry Taylor (designed by myself for Craft Supplies USA) are ideal for making small vessels out of tagua nut and similar materials (see page 28).

Timber and other materials

The original idea when I started this book was to make each box from a different wood. This proved to be totally impractical, but I did manage to use a large range of timbers, some home-grown, many of them imported exotics. I do not intend this chapter to be a comprehensive list of the timbers available, but rather a summary of my own experiences with the materials that I have used in the projects.

Fortunately, most boxes require relatively small pieces of wood; therefore any felled tree, or even prunings, can be looked on as possible box fodder. I once even made a small goblet from gooseberry wood. The most common branch wood used by turners is probably from the yew tree, one variety of which regularly produces long, almost straight branches which are cut off every few years to show off the trunk. Most of this material is probably from the Irish yew (*Taxus baccata* 'Fastigiata'), which has a more upright or columnar growth than the English variety. If you have access to a supply of these branches, you are indeed fortunate. Laburnum is another well-known tree that will provide excellent timber. Most of the fruitwoods – apple, pear, plum and almond – are delightful to turn, the latter two often showing interesting colour. Holly and boxwood are other garden trees that you will find superb to turn; being very fine-grained, they will take the finest detail, but in my experience they are the most difficult to season, frequently cracking up into pieces too small even for boxes. Ash and sycamore can provide material for the larger boxes. Ash is rather coarse-grained, while sycamore is rather soft. Maple can be quite fine-grained and harder, but often has a more cream-to-buff colour.

Ginger jar in yew (see no. 15)
h. 110mm (4¹¹/₃₂ in), d. 70mm (2³/₄ in)

Drying your own 'found' wood for boxes

The structure of wood is like a bundle of drinking straws, each straw (or column of cells) filled with moisture. When the 'straws' are cut across, the moisture escapes and the cells start to shrink and collapse. This causes the cracks in the end grain of a cut log or branch. The more this process is slowed, the better the prospect of saving sound wood. If the moisture is made to dissipate through the side grain instead, the cells can dry out in a much slower manner, resulting in far less degrade. This, you will appreciate, is a very simplistic explanation of the drying process, but over the years it has served me well enough. It should be remembered that, as a rough guide, air-drying planks of timber takes, on average, a year for each 25mm (1in) of thickness plus one more year.

My approach to drying branch wood has been to cut it into straight lengths and treat the end grain with hot candle wax, as soon as possible after cutting. The wax should be hot enough for the wood to sizzle when the end is dipped into it, and should set clear on the end grain. If it sets white or cloudy, the wood is not properly sealed. The lengths of wood then need to be put in a dry, airy place, but not with too much heat, as this would speed up the drying process and cause cracking. I have successfully dried yew up to 100mm (4in) in diameter in this manner. With laburnum, which is more dense, there is usually some cracking from the ends. It is always a long process, although the yew dries quite quickly. As an alternative to hot wax, which

carries a certain fire risk, there are several makes of PVA end-grain sealant on the market; these are particularly useful when dealing with larger sections of timber.

When preparing larger sections, such as logs, for box making, it is better to saw them into suitable-sized squares as soon as possible after felling, and wax the end grain in the same manner. If the sections are too big to wax, one of the PVA end-seal products available can be used instead.

Air-drying timber in this manner will only reduce the moisture content to 16–20%, which is not dry enough for the precise task of box making. Hence, the next step should be to move the partly dried timber into a warmer and drier place to lower the moisture content even further. Even then, turning boxes from branches can have its failures. There is always the risk that the stress left in the timber will cause it to split right to the centre pith. For larger boxes and vessels it is advisable to rough-turn first to reduce the bulk of material, and then allow the shapes to stabilize slowly.

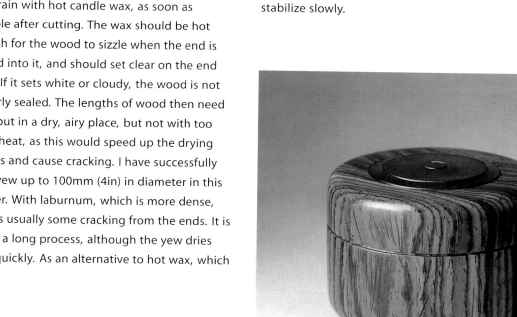

Round-cornered box in cocobolo with chattered ebony insert
h. 42mm (1²¹/₃₂in), d. 58mm (2⁹/₃₂in)

Exotic woods

Exotic timbers are frequently sold as 'part-seasoned'; this means that the moisture content can be anything from almost dry to wet through. Buyer beware! Exotic timbers in general, fortunately, do not 'move' much during the drying process, but it is always better to buy kiln-dried wood for boxes if it is available. Because of the difficulties in kilning exceptionally hard woods, there may be quite a large price difference between part-seasoned and kiln-dried. With the larger-diameter boxes, rough-turning will be advantageous. Starting with wood 50mm (2in) square – possibly the most popular size for small boxes – I would roughly round the timber, cut a spigot on each end and store it as long as possible before use.

NOTE: Exotic woods can be very brittle, so when preparing them for turning do not hammer the drive centre into the end grain – it can cause the timber to split.

I often nick the squares from corner to corner on the bandsaw, to give the four-point drive some purchase; this also ensures that the drive is central. A jig can be made to hold the squares in the correct position; I use my jig when sawing branches as well.

When buying exotic woods I look for suppliers who obtain their timber from sustainable sources – though, as with the naming of the timbers, you have only their word to go on. If we, as users of these woods, support only those suppliers who have a responsible attitude, we are in a way helping to ensure that the forests will be managed sympathetically, as well as creating employment in the country of origin. This will benefit us by ensuring that stocks of these timbers continue to be available in the future.

Having said that, remember that all woods can be quite variable from one tree to another. For this reason I would never buy timber without examining it carefully – certainly never by mail order.

There are a few other things to watch out for, such as cracks in the end grain; these are sometimes not easy to see, as the wood is usually waxed. To find good figure, examine the side grain: most of these timbers are quite straight-grained, so any ripples visible in the length will show up as figure on the finished pieces. Bubinga and purpleheart are usually very straight-grained, almost boring timbers,

Making a centre mark with the bandsaw, using a V-shaped cradle for support

The same cradle can be used when sawing branches to length

but I have seen them beautifully rippled. Knots will usually reduce the price of a length of timber, but there is always some more interesting grain around a knot. Tiny pin knots, on the other hand, are always worth watching out for as they will show up well in the finished work. Always look for the unusual – it will pay off in the end.

Burr or burl wood

In England the word *burr* is in common usage, as in 'burr elm', 'burr maple', etc. Americans prefer to say 'elm burl', 'maple burl' and so on. I quite happily use both terms and feel that they are interchangeable.

What is more important than the name is the fact that an abnormal growth on a tree can transform a common or even uninteresting wood into something extremely decorative and highly prized – and usually much more expensive.

What causes a burr is a question I have been asked many times. Whether it is caused by irritation or injury to the cells, no one seems to know for certain. My personal feeling is that it can be likened to a cancer: a proliferation of growth in one area of the tree. Any one of the 'eyes' could have developed into a branch, but in most cases they do not. However, you cannot tell a customer that you are selling them a piece of cancerous growth, can you?

**Burr yew vessel with Danish oil finish
h. 279mm (11in)**

Notes on the timbers used in the 50 boxes

Botanical names and alternative trade names for these timbers have been given where possible, but usage may vary from one supplier to another, and for the rarer woods reliable information is difficult to come by.

ACACIA (*Robinia pseudoacacia*) Properly known as **false acacia**, or (especially in USA) **locust**. Yellow to golden-brown, sapwood white, can be fumed to an olive green. Fairly coarse grain but finishes easily. **Acacia burl** is easier to turn, cuts easily even with a scraper – one of my favourite home-grown woods.

AFRICAN TEAK (*Strychnos atherstonei*) Red to brown. Quite hard but finishes easily. Dust is irritant – made me sneeze violently.

AMARELLO (*Aspidosperma* spp.) Properly called **pequiá amarelo**. Bright yellow. Easy to turn but very prone to heat-checking.

AMAZAQUE (*Guibourtia ehie*) Also called **amazakoue**, **hyedua** or **ovangkol**. This can be rather like grey walnut, but frequently has a lustre. Turns very well – one of the easy exotics.

ASH (*Fraxinus excelsior*) Mainly white. Coarse grain, turns well, available in large sizes. **Rippled ash** is figured at right angles to the grain direction, and very decorative. Timber from older trees can develop a brown coloration, known as **olive ash**; this can be very variable in density, but finishes easily. **American ash** (*F. americana*) is usually harder and whiter than European, but is not always available.

BEECH (*Fagus sylvatica*), **SPALTED** The common beech infected with fungus. Very decorative black markings. Extremely variable, can have soft areas. Dust is always to be regarded as hazardous.

BIRD'S-EYE MAPLE (*Acer saccharum*) Highly figured, though the 'eyes' only show on tangentially cut faces. Turns well.

BLOODWOOD, SATINÉ (*Brosimum paraense*) Deep red with a yellow lustre. Very hard, finishes very well.

BOX ELDER BURL (*Acer negundo*) Belongs to the maple family. Cream, sometimes has pink streaks. Quite soft, superb figure. Turns easily with some tear-out.

Inset-lid box in ebony and amarello (see no. 37)
h. 76mm (3in), d. 50mm (1$^{31}/_{32}$in)

BOXWOOD (*Buxus sempervirens*) Creamy-yellow. Difficult to dry. Cuts beautifully, finishes well.

BUBINGA (*Guibourtia demeusii*) Red to brown with pink or reddish stripes, sometimes nicely figured. Easy to work.

BUDGIEROO (botanical name unknown) New to me. Dark tan colour, not very striking. Turns very easily.

CAMPHOR (*Cinnamomum camphora*) Also called **camphor laurel**. Cream to pink with reddish-black streaks. Coarse grain, powerful smell.

CHITTAM BURL (probably *Cotinus americana*) Deep yellow, very lustrous. Very expensive and rare; I only use it as an insert. I understand it is a root burl on a tree that grows in rocky places, and that harvesting is done with dynamite rather than a chainsaw!

COCOBOLO (*Dalbergia retusa*) One of the most colourful of all the rosewoods, very dense and oily. Easy enough to turn, but quickly clogs abrasive; I always use my wax-lubricated sanding technique (see page 40) to overcome this. Dust can be very irritant.

EBONY, black (*Diospyros crassiflora*) Usually fine-grained and easy to turn, but the timber is imported from many sources, and so can vary somewhat in the way it turns and finishes. **Asian ebony** (*D. discolor*) may have streaks of lighter colour, sometimes with a greenish tinge, and turns very easily. Dust can be irritant. **Macassar ebony** (*D. macassar* or *D. celebica*) can have very marked stripes, sometimes almost cream, with black; very striking, but variable.

ELM BURR (*Ulmus* spp.) Almost a lost species. Extremely variable in pattern and scale of figure. Rather coarse grain for boxes.

EUCALYPTUS BURL (*Eucalyptus regnans* and others) Many varieties available, varying from quite soft to exceptionally hard. Usually very decorative. Liable to 'move' a great deal during the drying process.

GONÇALO ALVES (*Astronium fraxinifolium*) Other names include **zebrawood**, **tigerwood**, **locustwood**. Dark tan colour with chocolate streaks; variable – some samples have no streaks. Turns quite easily, especially when kiln-dried.

HOLLY (*Ilex aquifolium*) White, very fine texture. One of the most difficult home-grown timbers to dry, but a joy to turn.

IMBUYA (*Phoebe porosa*) Pale, warm brown, but can have some darker markings. Some samples have been rather fibrous. In general it turns easily, but needs care to achieve a good finish on the end grain. I have some which is hard and dense, and is much easier to finish. Smells of nutmeg.

Straight-sided box in cocobolo with chittam burl insert h. 42mm (1²¹/₃₂in), d. 61mm (2¹³/₃₂in)

A variant of the Yew box (see no. 10) in maple burr and karanda
h. 70mm (2³/₄in), d. 72mm (2²⁷/₃₂in)

INDIAN ROSEWOOD (*Dalbergia latifolia*) Not often available. Reddish-purple in colour, turns and finishes very nicely. The same species is plantation-grown and marketed as **sonokeling**.

KARANDA (*Prosopis kuntzei*) Extremely hard, heavy, slightly fibrous and lustrous timber; not easy to work, but finishes like glass. Dusky purple colour.

KINGWOOD (*Dalbergia cearensis*) Pale to deep purple with darker lines. Lustrous. Very fine-grained, nice to work.

LABURNUM (*Laburnum vulgare*) Nice contrast between the dark brown heart and the whitish sapwood. Quite hard but turns and finishes well.

LEADWOOD (*Combretum imbrebe*) Another very dense timber, dark grey to black, fine-grained, and finishes extremely well.

LILAC (*Syringa vulgaris*) Usually cream, but can have pale purple streaks in it. Never grows to more than a small ornamental tree. However, it is one of the hardest English-grown timbers, and probably one of the most difficult to dry in anything but small sections. I usually cut it into the largest squares I can (excluding the heart), keep it in a cool place, and hope for the best. It is, however, one of the most beautiful woods to turn.

MAHOGANY (*Swietenia macrophylla* and others) 'Mahogany' is probably the most variable of all imported timbers, because many entirely different species are sold under the same name. If I buy it I look for the darkest, heaviest piece.

MAPLE (*Acer* spp.) A very large family of trees; the **English** or **field maple** (*A. campestre*) is a cream-to-buff colour, fairly fine-grained, and quite good for the larger box. Some of the American maples can be even better, being whiter and much harder.

MAPLE BURL (*Acer* spp). The sample I used came from a bigleaf maple (*A. macrophyllum*) from western USA. Quite soft and easy to work, but may need filling to achieve a good finish.

MASUR BIRCH (*Betula* spp.) Very highly figured timber from Finland (not a distinct species), usually available in small logs. When buying, make sure the figure goes all the way round. Gives spectacular results when turned end-grain.

MEXICAN ROSEWOOD (*Cordia gerascanthus* or *C. elaeagnoides*) Also called **bocote**, and not a true rosewood, but still a nice timber for boxes. I prefer the pale-coloured pieces, as these are softer and easier to work. The darker, harder samples can go almost black quite quickly.

OLIVEWOOD (*Olea europaea*) Cream to pale brown with darker markings. Can be very highly figured, always extremely oily, and clogs the abrasive. Use the wax-lubricated sanding technique (see page 40). It is difficult to achieve a shine on olive, as the oil tends to absorb a wax finish.

OSAGE ORANGE (*Maclura aurantiaca* or *Toxylon pomiferum*) A superb wood for boxes. Bright yellow colour, which unfortunately mellows to a dark tan eventually.

PADAUK (*Pterocarpus soyauxii*) Bright red, but unfortunately soon darkens to a rich brown. Easy to work. The dye stains collars and cuffs, the dust can be irritating.

PARAKINGWOOD (*Dalbergia pacifica*) Sometimes called **Mexican kingwood**. Looks like a purple cocobolo and is very decorative. Like all the rosewoods, it turns and finishes beautifully.

PEAR (*Pyrus communis*), **STEAMED** Common pearwood, steamed during the drying process, turns a pale pinkish colour. Turns and finishes very easily.

PERNAMBUCO (*Caesalpina echinata* or *Guilandina echinata*) Deep orange, turning darker with age, sometimes lustrous. Hard and heavy. Often difficult to work, but finishes well.

PINK IVORY (*Rhamnus zeyheri* or *Berchemia zeyheri*) Also known as **red ivory**. I always pick out the palest pieces, as these seem to keep their colour longer. The redder samples can be coarser and turn brown readily. A superb wood to turn, but liable to heat checks.

Spear-topped variation of the Onion-top box (see no. 3), in padauk
h. 85mm (3¹¹/₃₂in), d. 47mm (1²⁷/₃₂in)

PURPLEHEART (*Peltogyne venosa*) Also known as **amaranth**. Hard, dense timber. Brown when first cut, and needs a few days in the sun to bring up the colour. Gradually turns brown with age. Some samples have resin lines in the growth rings; avoid these. I have come across specimens with a lovely ripple in the grain, which is worth watching out for.

Pill box in ebony and pink ivory (see no. 13)
h. 33mm (1⁵/₁₆in), d. 44mm (1³/₄in)

PUTUMUJU (*Centrolobium* spp.) A beautiful wood, yellow to orange, sometimes with red streaks. Fine-grained, and available in larger sizes; an excellent timber.

RIO ROSEWOOD (*Dalbergia nigra*) Import of this wood is now banned, but there is still some old stock available. Almost black with purple streaks. Beautiful smell when worked.

SANTOS ROSEWOOD (*Machaerium scleroxylon*) Not a true rosewood. Mid-brown with darker patches. Turns very well, but the dust affects some people.

SATINWOOD (*Chloroxylon swietenia*) A lustrous, yellow, slightly coarse-grained wood from Sri Lanka; the figure only shows along the grain. Smells of coconut when turned.

SHE-OAK (*Allocasuarina fraserana*) Warm, brown wood with distinct rays, good for larger boxes.

SNAKEWOOD (*Brosimum guianensis* or *B. aubletti* syn. *Piratinera guianensis*) Rich brown with darker markings. Rare and expensive. One of the heaviest woods available, also one of the most decorative. Some logs have no figure, so do not buy without close inspection. It cuts almost like plastic, but is very brittle and can crack readily.

SONOKELING (*Dalbergia latifolia*) Botanically the same as **Indian rosewood**, but plantation-grown, which makes it softer and more colourful. Easy to work, but may need extra coats of sealer to achieve a good finish.

SYCAMORE (*Acer pseudoplatanus*) White-to-cream wood; if not end-reared soon after sawing, it can develop grey-to-blue streaks. Sometimes has a wavy grain and is then known as **rippled** or **fiddleback sycamore**. Easy to work, but rather soft for small boxes. Note that in American usage the name 'sycamore' is applied to the American plane tree, *Platanus occidentalis*, whose wood is similar to the London plane (*P.* x *hispanica* syn. *P.* x *acerifolia*).

SYRINGA (botanical name uncertain) A timber new to me. My sample has greenish-grey streaks, with a whitish sapwood. Slightly coarse grain, easy to cut but needs care in finishing. I would not buy it again.

THUYA BURR (*Tetraclinis articulata*) One of the most beautiful burrs available. Very resinous, so needs care in cutting and finishing.

TULIPWOOD, BRAZILIAN (*Dalbergia frutescens*) A superb rosewood, straw-coloured with red-to-crimson lines, but the colour can vary greatly. Not to be confused with tulip tree or yellow poplar (*Liriodendron tulipifera*), which is entirely unrelated.

VIOLET ROSEWOOD (*Dalbergia louvelli*) Deep purple, sometimes with black streaks. A very dense wood that cuts and finishes very well. Unfortunately it soon darkens on exposure to sunlight.

Pill box variation in snakewood with beaded lid (see no. 13)
h. 27mm (1¹/₁₆ in), d. 46mm (1¹³/₁₆ in)

YEW (*Taxus baccata*) One of the most colourful English woods: the orange heartwood and white sapwood provide a superb contrast which can be used to good effect in boxes. Sand with care to avoid heat-checking. Dust from this species can be hazardous.

ZEBRANO (*Microberlinia brazzavillensis*) A quite coarse-grained wood with some lustre; the pale and dark brown stripes can be used to good effect in some boxes. However, the strong grain pattern can easily overpower some box designs.

ZIRICOTE (*Cordia dodecandra*) Grey-brown with random black lines. Hard and heavy. Turns well, if rather dusty – a bit like turning coal.

Zebrano box with one-piece lid (see no. 9)
h. 75mm (2³¹/₃₂in), d. 44mm (1³/₄in)

Other vegetable materials

BAMBOO (*Bambusa* spp. and others) Sections of this have been used as containers from primitive times. It does need some care when turning, as it is very fibrous. If larger sizes can be found, it has some interesting possibilities.

GRASS-TREE ROOT (*Xanthorrhoea* spp.) Not a true wood, it is actually one of the lily family. It is usually turned into larger vessels; however, if a lid is added this creates a box.

Lidded vessel in grass-tree root
h. 100mm (3¹⁵/₁₆in), d. 140mm (5³³/₆₄in)

Cylindrical box in bamboo with pernambuco inserts
h. 57mm (2¹/₄in) , d. 31mm (1⁷/₃₂in)

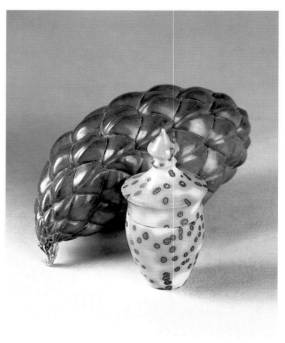

Two mini-bottles in tagua nut with wooden tops
Left: **ebony top, h. 39mm (1³⁵⁄₆₄in), d. 21mm (⁵³⁄₆₄in)**
Right: **cocobolo top, h. 52mm (2¹⁄₁₆in), d. 31mm (1⁷⁄₃₂in)**

Lidded jar in thika pod
h. 60mm (2³⁄₈in), d. 29mm (1⁵⁄₃₂in)

TAGUA NUT (*Altua tagua*) An almost round nut about 25mm (1in) in diameter, always with a void in the centre. Useful for miniature vessels, or inlays.

THIKA PODS (botanical name unknown) The nut inside these pods is an unusual turquoise-to-green colour, with reddish-brown flecks. Turns easily. The empty pod could also be used to create a box or vessel.

UXI NUT (*Raphia taegiadia*) A smaller nut than tagua, with brown-to-black flecks throughout, also suitable for miniature vessels or inlays.

Artificial materials

The various resin-based materials are available in solid squares or bars, as well as in sheet form for inlay work. I find them easier to turn using scraping techniques. Reduce the speed for sanding, and polish with a commercial metal polish or similar. These materials respond really well to final finishing with the buffing system.

Ginger jar (see no. 15) in uxi nut
h. 32mm (1¹⁷⁄₆₄in), d. 21mm (⁵³⁄₆₄in)

Box in green and yellow cast resin
h. 44mm (1⁴⁷/₆₄in), d. 39mm (1¹⁷/₃₂in)

Real abalone shell

Box with chatterwork lid in blue cast resin
h. 21mm (⁵³/₆₄in), d. 41mm (1⁵/₈in)

ABALONE SHELL ALTERNATIVE The real thing
may not be easy to find, but the alternative
variety is readily available.

COLOURED CAST RESIN I found two different
makes on sale in America; both are semi-
translucent and available in a range of
colours, with the yellow and green
especially striking. These materials need
particular care when cutting, as the slightest
dig-in can result in the piece shattering.

IVORY ALTERNATIVE Made from a cast polyester
resin, and available in many sizes. Turns
reasonably well (with care), takes a high
shine, and does not discolour with age.

Box in alternative ivory, with chatterwork insert in
pink ivory wood
h. 45mm (1²⁵/₃₂in), d. 52mm (2¹/₁₆in)

METAL TUBE Aluminium or brass tube can be used to make a useful box. For the example shown here, I used my Superthin parting tool to separate the piece for the lid. The material needs to be well supported during turning, and a file was needed to clean up the cut surfaces.

MOTHER-OF-PEARL ALTERNATIVE My example was cut from a piece of thin inlay material, which was all I had. A slice cut from a solid block would have allowed for a more attractive curved surface.

TORTOISESHELL ALTERNATIVE Like ivory alternative but translucent. Makes a very attractive box.

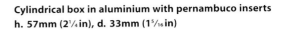

Cylindrical box in aluminium with pernambuco inserts
h. 57mm (2¹⁄₄ in), d. 33mm (1⁵⁄₁₆ in)

Box in tortoiseshell alternative
h. 35mm (1³⁄₈ in), d. 48mm (1⁷⁄₈ in)

Mother-of-pearl and abalone alternatives

Deciding what to make

For the hobbyist working alone in the shed, deciding what to make is a relatively simple matter, depending only on individual ability and the materials available. The time taken to create an item, and the cost of the wood, are frequently ignored; what matters is the creative process.

For the commercial turner, the question of what to make is a rather more complex affair. Market forces will dictate, to some extent, how the work is done and what is produced. When I was turning commercially I based my choice of design on two main factors: target market and intended use.

Target market

Does the turner choose to make items for the craft-fair market, or for the gallery and collectors' market? I have simplified the possibilities into just these two areas. In reality, of course, there are several areas. Competitions and exhibitions require the same sort of products as the galleries, where quality and originality are very important factors, whereas in a souvenir or gift shop the products would be similar to those required at a craft fair, where price is most definitely a consideration. This does not mean that poorly made boxes will sell at these venues – a well-made product is still the aim.

Two boxes in sycamore with ebony finials, and one in Masur birch
all approx. 100mm (4in) high

Craft-fair boxes

For this market moderate prices seem to work best, as many potential customers have price barriers. In order to keep the cost reasonable, the boxes must be quick to make – it is no good selling an item for £5 or $10 if it took you two hours to make it. Therefore the most sensible box design, if speed of making is a major consideration, is one where the lid projects down into the base. This means that the lid can be completed at the same time as the box and then just parted off from the base. This requires only one chucking operation and therefore saves a lot of time.

As in life, a solution often creates another problem. Here, the problem is that the lid is solid but the base is hollowed, and the two will expand or contract at different rates. Timber is a living material, and whenever we cut it we are relieving stresses within it, which will make it warp to some extent. The solution to this problem is to leave the lids with an easy fit, that is, slightly loose. Hence these pieces cannot be called pill boxes, but they can be called ring boxes. They can be displayed on a dressing table to hold a favourite ring or other precious object. The loose lid can now be seen as an advantage, as the box can be opened with one hand. Also, by calling them 'ring boxes', the customer is given a reason to buy them.

Gallery or collectors' boxes

The distinction I draw between craft-fair and gallery boxes is only arbitrary; many of the former could, with a little thought and time, have the undersides of their lids turned, and made to fit snugly into the bases. Many, if not most, of the designs put forward in this book could not be made using the craft-fair methods: it would, for example, be totally unacceptable to make the Apple box (no. 23) with the top half solid. Therefore for the gallery market it virtually has to be accepted that the top and base are chucked and turned separately.

This opens up new possibilities, as the lid and base can be of contrasting woods, hopefully adding to the appeal of the design. The technique of 'jam'-chucking (see pages 64–7) becomes an essential part of box making, allowing you to hold either lid or base on a waste block in order to complete the other side to the same standard as the rest of the project. All this extra work means that the box will take longer to make and will therefore have to cost more.

Intended use

The intended use of the box will also be an important deciding factor, as the degree of fit of the lid is very relevant to the design selected. Any item made for sale must be suitable for its intended market.

- A lidded bowl intended for sugar, for example, needs a loose-fitting lid. The user can then open it with one hand. Loose-fitting lids tend to be quicker to make.
- If the box is to be regularly carried in a pocket or handbag, as with a pill box, it will need a tight lid in order to be functional, and will tend to take longer to make.

From the above criteria other decisions will flow, such as choice of timber, finish and originality.

The plans provided in this book will show some of the ideas that have developed for me, personally, from the above decision-making process. These boxes, if practised, should provide a good starting point for the near-limitless

Two views of a flared-top box with chattered top, in ziricote
h. 44mm (1³/₄ in), d. 57mm (2¹/₄ in)

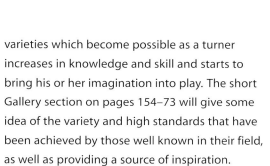

varieties which become possible as a turner increases in knowledge and skill and starts to bring his or her imagination into play. The short Gallery section on pages 154–73 will give some idea of the variety and high standards that have been achieved by those well known in their field, as well as providing a source of inspiration.

Inspiration and where to find it

Inspiration from ceramics: two views of a Ginger jar in rippled ash (see no. 15)
h. 114mm (4¹/₂ in), d. 73mm (2⁷/₈ in)

We do not have to sit like Rodin's *Thinker* and wait for inspiration to strike – ideas are everywhere. Many of the designs in this book are taken from everyday images: a cylinder, a sphere – I could have added a cube and a cone – all simple geometric shapes that we see around us. From nature come many more ideas: an egg, a teardrop, an apple, a pear, an acorn. It is just a matter of looking at things in a different light. Converting these images into a box form takes a little more imagination, but that is all part of the fun of making boxes.

I have not even touched on the many 'practical' boxes that could be made: sugar bowls, jam pots, needle cases, perfume holders, and many others, like condiment sets (these are maybe out of fashion these days, but still useful for picnics and alfresco meals, since they are more or less unbreakable). The one thing they all have in common is that box-making techniques are needed to make them.

If your tastes are more traditional, look at containers made in other materials, such as glass or ceramics, for inspiration. One good source of shapes is the perfume or cosmetics department in your local store. The manufacturers pay a fortune to have a special, distinctive container designed to show off their products, and you can 'borrow' suggestions from these for free. In case you feel shy about hanging round these departments, the containers are often featured in the catalogues that many stores distribute at Christmas.

One of the ideas behind compiling this series of designs is to show that there are so many variations to each concept, and so many woods available, that unless you wish to, you never have to turn two boxes alike.

Decorating boxes

Grain and figure

Since almost all these boxes are turned in end grain – that is, with the grain of the wood running parallel to the lathe bed – some timbers will inevitably cause disappointment. Woods like zebrano or tulipwood have a strongly coloured grain which shows up as well on the top surface of a turned box as it does on the side. Spalted beech can sometimes show an even more interesting pattern on the end grain than on the side. However, many woods which show a superb figure on the side grain are uninteresting, to the point of being boring, on the end grain – an effect which reminds me of the old saying 'a twopenny head and a farthing tail'. Two that come to mind are satinwood from Sri Lanka and bird's-eye maple. In the case of the latter, the only surface that shows the 'eyes' is at right angles to the grain. Woods like this require a little careful thought in order to show them off to their best advantage.

To make the most of a wood like bird's-eye maple I would turn a box with the grain oriented like a bowl blank, showing cross grain on the top surface rather than end grain. The top needs to be as flat as possible to show off the grain, so a design such as the UFO box (no. 33) would be suitable. This also has the effect of reducing the amount of the very plain end grain showing. Achieving a good finish when hollowing the side grain is more difficult and can require some sophisticated tools, so in this design I have made the opening minimal, like a small bowl, and fitted

Box in spalted beech, with insert between box and lid to ensure grain match
h. 68mm (2^{11}/$_{16}$ in), d. 70mm (2^{3}/$_{4}$ in)

a top made from a contrasting wood to complete the effect. This is one case where I have had to let the wood dictate the design to some extent.

Beads and grooves

The easiest way of making a plain surface more attractive is to apply some sort of decorative feature. Creating beads or grooves gives the surface shadows and highlights, which will effectively break up a plain expanse. Beads on boxes need to be extremely small, often about 1.5mm (^{1}/$_{16}$ in), otherwise they will overpower the design. I create small beads such as these with the 3mm (^{1}/$_{8}$ in) parting tool, first cutting a square fillet and then

Round-edge box with beaded and chattered top, in violet rosewood
h. 52mm (2¹/₁₆ in), d. 49mm (1¹⁵/₁₆ in)

removing the corners. After sanding, I have a simple raised bead. This can be on the top surface of a box, forming a ring, or it can project from the side.

Grooves are cut either with the corner of a parting tool or with the long point of the skew chisel, used flat like a scraper. The tools must be very sharp to avoid tear-out of the grain. Two grooves cut very close together will look, after sanding, like an inset bead.

Whether you use beads or grooves, they both serve the same purpose of visually breaking up a plain surface, or focusing the eye on a feature. However, it is very easy to overdo the effect and make the item too fussy. A good guide is: decorate a plain wood, keep a figured wood simple.

Lid insert in green and yellow resin with chatterwork

Chatterwork

This very useful technique is only effective on end grain, and so is eminently suitable for decorating the tops of boxes. It is created by applying a sharpened spring-steel tool to the surface of the work, the effect being governed by the length of tool overhanging the toolrest, the degree of pressure, and the length of blade extended from the holder. The tool I use is one designed by Dennis Stewart, which came with the original set of hollowing tools bearing his name. I grind the end of the blade to a slight curve, then use a diamond hone to polish the cutting edge and remove the burr.

The width between the chatter marks is dependent on the speed of rotation, which also varies with the diameter of the wood. Before chattering a finished article in an unfamiliar wood, I usually experiment to find the optimum speed for the effect I want. To create chatter I set the speed of the lathe at around 1,400rpm for a diameter of about 38mm (1¹/₂in), angle the tool downwards and gradually apply it to the surface. The screaming

The Dennis Stewart chatter tool

Straight-sided box in boxwood with offset inserts in purpleheart, holly and ebony
h. 39mm (1¹⁷/₃₂in), d. 48mm (1⁷/₈in)

I frequently inlay discs using my picture-frame technique, described on page 140. The beauty of this is that it keeps the lid thin, and also shows the original colour of the timber on the inside. This idea can be used for any sample of wood showing exceptional colour or grain pattern.

I have experienced no problems when inserting an end-grain inlay into end grain. With a side-grain insert into an end-grain box there is a greater risk of movement, so I make sure that the insert is as dry as possible.

Inlaying rings

In the top

Cutting the groove accurately can be a little tricky because two diameters – the inside and outside of the ring – have to be perfectly matched. Remember also that the ring is to fit into the top surface of the box without showing on the inside, and that the finished thickness of the top needs to be very shallow – generally no more than 3mm (¹/₈in). This means that the ring must be no more than 1.5mm (¹/₁₆in) thick when the lid is finished.

The way I approach this is to cut the ring first, a little deeper than needed, from a contrasting timber. I create the lid in the usual way, leaving the top a little thicker than normal. Using the 3mm (¹/₈in) parting tool, I cut a spigot on the top surface to match the inside diameter of the ring. Once the ring fits snugly on to this spigot I can extend this cut down into the lid and widen the slot until it matches the outside diameter of the ring. After gluing the ring in place, a final cut can be made across the top of the lid to level the surface. With a slight variation of this technique I can leave a small contrasting bead proud of the

sound that this produces is a good indication that the tool is chattering the surface. If the end of the blade is on the centre line, then the marks will be radial – that is, each mark will lie on a radius. However, if the tool is above or below the centre line the marks are angled and can give a spiral effect. I usually define the chattered area with either grooves or beads, to focus the eye on the decorated area. Note that I find it essential to sand the end grain before applying the chatterwork.

Inlays

Inlaying a ring or disc of contrasting wood into the top can make a world of difference to the appearance of any box. This technique can be used to improve unattractive end grain, or to make exceptional pieces of wood go further by cutting them into slices and then inlaying into a more mundane box. Often I come across tiny patches of burr (burl) too small to use for anything else. I cut these into 6mm (¹/₄in) slices and dry them in the microwave oven (about 10 minutes on 'defrost' is a safe starting point), allow them to cool, and repeat until bone dry. There may be some warping, but usually not enough to worry about. When cut into a small disc and glued to a waste block mounted in the chuck, they are ready for inlaying.

surface. If you do not have a tool small enough to cut such a narrow slot, you can make one from a hardened nail and fit it into a handle, or grind the end of a small screwdriver to do the job.

In the side

Inserting a ring of contrasting wood into the side of a box requires some very careful measuring and cutting. With this technique I cut the slot first, usually with my Superthin parting tool. Then I measure the diameter in the bottom of the slot, using my cheap vernier callipers. The jaws on these are only 1mm (just over $^1/_{32}$in) wide so they will fit into very narrow spaces.

A ring of the contrasting wood is needed, with its inside diameter matching this measurement. The thickness of the ring has to be a close fit in the groove. The outside diameter is not critical as long as the width of the ring is equal to the depth of the groove, or slightly more if a contrasting bead is required. The main difficulty now is to part it off

cleanly – it is very easy to leave some whiskers on the edge of the ring, which would prevent it from going in the slot. To overcome this I grind the lower bevel of my Superthin parting tool at a slight angle, with the right-hand edge forward; this ensures that the breakthrough is on the edge of the ring and the chance of whiskers is minimized. Now break the ring and spring it over the box and into the slot; if everything has been measured and cut correctly, the broken edges should meet perfectly. The ring can now be glued in place, and a final skim taken down the side of the box. If the box is of such a shape that the ring cannot be sprung over the end, then two breaks will be necessary.

Inserts and rings do not have to be just wood. There are several alternatives available: alternative ivory, mother-of-pearl, tagua-nut slices, even coins (these could commemorate a special date); there are also several cabochons of semiprecious stone available. I have even seen metals such as pewter set into box lids.

A selection of stone cabochons which can be used as lid inserts

Finishes for boxes

The choice of finish and the technique used will depend on the final use of the article and the market in which it will be sold. All need the sanding process, but deciding what to use afterwards needs thought – and the experience of listening to customers' requirements. I have indicated below what my customers have taught me about their preferences.

The finishing process starts the minute you put down the gouge or scraper. Once the shape is completed, the surface of the wood needs to be made as flawless as possible. In practice, when making boxes, this is not all done at the end: the inside of the lid, for example, has to be completed before it is reverse-chucked for the top to be turned. However, the process at each stage is the same, and this is sanding.

Bell-shaped box with chattered lid, in cocobolo h. 48mm (1⁷⁄₈in), d. 60mm (2³⁄₈in)

Sanding

For a coarser abrasive I generally use a waterproof cloth-backed material made in Germany. For the finer grits, from 400 to 2000, I use a wet-and-dry paper which is produced for the motor-finishing trade and is very consistent in quality. I never use glasspaper or garnet paper, which are really made for cabinetmakers and do not stand up well to the relatively high speeds of woodturning.

The first grit used should be coarse enough to remove any turning marks quickly with only a couple of wipes over before moving on to the next finer grit. As your toolwork improves, you will find that you need less and less of the coarser grits. I find, these days, that I can happily start with 240 grit in most cases. (In my early days I was using 120 grit.)

This is followed by 320 and 400. After the 400 you need to check the surface for any residual scratches – in fact, it is better to check before each change of grit. The basic problem is that woodturners inevitably sand across the grain and this always creates scratches. The cabinetmaker always sands with the grain and invariably needs nothing finer than 240 grit to complete the work.

The scratches from 400 grit may be plainly visible on many of the harder, close-grained woods that we use. In fact, with ebony I will often sand down to 1200 or 1500 grit to ensure that no scratches are visible to the naked eye. This is where a strong raking light helps, as the reflected light on the surface of the wood shows up scratches that may not be otherwise easily apparent.

With some woods that have a high oil or resin content, such as olive and cocobolo, the abrasive clogs up almost immediately. In these cases I use

discs of various grits. Once again, overheating the pad or the wood is to be avoided. A very light touch helps to reduce overheating; it allows the grit to cut and shed the dust, as opposed to pressing the pad into the surface, which makes the pad clog up and create more heat. Even so, I would still finish off by hand-sanding using finer grits.

Sealing

I have always used cellulose sanding sealer as opposed to spirit-based sealer or friction polish. This is because in my craft-fair days I needed a sealer that would dry almost instantly, to get sufficient throughput of production. A spirit-based sealer takes around 15 minutes to dry totally before it can be sanded again, whereas the cellulose can be friction-dried and sanded almost immediately.

I use sanding sealer in preference to a surface treatment (such as melamine lacquer or friction polish) because I want the finish *in* the wood rather than *on* the wood. Frequently, to achieve the ultimate finish on more open-grained woods such as padauk or zebrano, I will apply sanding sealer between each grit. This will gradually fill up the grain with sealer and create a much better shine.

To apply sealer I have always used a brush, flooding it on in a slightly thinned state (thinned with cellulose thinners to the consistency of single cream). If used neat, straight from the can, I find it far too thick: it dries before I can wipe it off the surface. Using it diluted is a compromise between filling the grain quickly and speed of operation. Once brushed on, I wipe the surplus off with a paper towel almost immediately. Then with a dry piece of towel I friction-dry the surface. The wood is then ready for further sanding or for the next stage of finishing.

what I call 'wax-lubricated sanding'. This means applying a very soft paste wax to the abrasive and sanding at low speed to avoid throwing liquid wax all over the workshop. Even after this process, cellulose can still be used, because it will cut through the wax and still seal the wood.

It is always a good idea to drop the speed when sanding, to reduce any problems created by overheating the wood. Many woods, including yew and amarello, are very susceptible to heat-checking, and others are to a lesser degree. Heat-checking is where little cracks develop at right angles to the grain, and as woodturners are frequently sanding very thin areas of end grain it is all too easy to 'overcook' the wood.

My philosophy with sanding is that 'The shine should always be on the wood before it is sealed in.' No amount of applied finish will disguise sanding scratches or tool marks.

Power sanding

I occasionally make large vessels or lidded bowls which are technically boxes or containers, and for these power sanding is a sensible and speedy option. I use an ordinary electric drill, at high speed, with a soft Velcro pad attachment which carries

Waxing

When I was doing the craft fairs I found that the customers very much liked to see a high shine on boxes, so I used pure carnauba wax melted onto the wood surface. This is achieved by pressing a solid block of wax onto the rotating item; the friction will melt the wax. The knack is to get an even layer over all the surface; I do this by spreading it using fingers and a paper towel. Too much pressure and you will wipe it all off; not enough, and the surface will be streaky. The item can then be brought to a high shine using light pressure from the paper. Even now that I no longer do 'production' work, I still use carnauba wax on small items that require a high shine.

It can be quite tricky to get used to carnauba wax, because if you don't press hard enough you will leave rings, and if you press too hard you wipe it all off again. I learnt the hard way that if carnauba is applied too thickly it has a tendency to flake off after the box is sold, and customers, naturally enough, do not like this.

Galleries usually appreciate a softer shine than the carnauba-wax finish, so these days, when doing 'posh pots', I use a very quick-drying soft wax, such as Briwax, applied with 0000 steel wool, or the finest Webrax, to avoid getting too much of a build-up and remove any sealer left on the surface. (Webrax is a trade name for a non-woven nylon material impregnated with abrasive, available in various 'grits'. Its main advantage is

that it does not break down like steel wool.) I then buff with a dry paper towel. On the insides of boxes this is the final surface.

Buffing

On a demonstrating trip to America I came across the Beall polishing system, which consists of three buffing wheels, two polishing compounds and pure carnauba wax, along with a mandrel for fitting on the lathe. I found it was too expensive to import into Britain, so I sourced all the components locally for my own polishing kit. This comprises three buffing wheels marked 1, 2 and 3; blocks of tripoli and white lustre compound; carnauba wax; and a pigtail mandrel which fits into a Jacobs chuck in the lathe headstock. I now use the following system to finish the outsides of all my boxes:

1   With the first wheel mounted on the lathe, I apply tripoli compound to the surface of the wheel and buff the whole of the outside of the box with a light touch, buffing in the direction of the grain wherever possible. This removes any fine scratches that may still be lurking. Tripoli is an abrasive and it has to be used sensibly, as the surface can be scoured if it is applied too heavily. Also, if the box is pressed on too hard it can be torn from the hand and hurled across the workshop. This is a mistake that I remember every time it happens, and it wastes an hour's work and a piece of good wood.

2   The wheel marked 2 is then mounted, and a minimal amount of white lustre compound applied to it. The surface of the box is buffed again, removing any surplus tripoli and creating a deep shine on the wood.

The Chris Stott polishing kit

3 The final buffing wheel, marked 3, has the carnauba wax wiped quickly across its surface, and the box is again applied to the wheel. This final process polishes the wood itself, and results in a far better shine than anything applied to the surface can achieve.

I find that this treatment shows off the grain of the wood to its best advantage. Because there is only a minimal amount of residual wax on the surface, the boxes are less likely to be marked with fingers. If they do eventually get marked they can always be buffed up again, which can be handy before an exhibition or show, or as a way of reviving last year's stock.

Oil

I occasionally use Danish oil as a sealer to finish a larger box or lidded vessel if I feel that the oil would show off the figure better, or if the item is to be used for food storage, as with a sugar bowl. Woods like yew respond well to the oiling process, though it is messy and comparatively slow.

I apply oil to the wood with a brush when the lathe is stationary, wait a few minutes for some to soak in, and then wipe off the surplus and buff dry with a paper towel. Danish oil takes at least four hours to dry, but I leave it overnight. A second coat is usually needed and, if the grain has lifted at all, the surface needs sanding first. I will often wet-sand at this stage: I apply a coat of oil and, with the lathe running slowly, sand with a very fine abrasive – 800 or even 1000 grit, depending on the timber. Any remaining slurry can be removed with more oil, and the surface buffed with paper towels until it feels dry.

A shine may take anything from two to four applications, depending on the wood. Softer woods are often more absorbent, and so take more oil to give a good depth of shine. After the applications of oil I prefer to leave the box to harden off for at least a week. It can then go through the buffing process, or be hand-polished with soft wax.

Varnish

For a more waterproof finish, I have in the past used polyurethane varnish, thinned slightly with turpentine substitute and applied in exactly the same way as Danish oil.

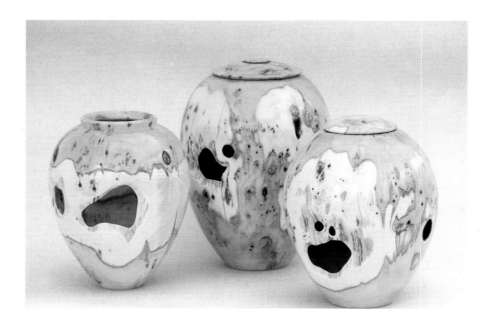

Burr yew vessels with Danish oil finish
h. 228–279mm (9–11in)

Displaying your work

Displaying the work to advantage is another important factor when trying to tempt a potential customer. It is all right to look down at a range of bowls, but the smaller items need to be seen closer to eye level. I made a stand from chrome towel rail that had 15 teardrop-shaped Perspex shelves. Each shelf could carry three boxes of different designs, all made from the same wood. This stand was always placed in a strategic position and brightly lit with spotlights.

This certainly paid off, because customers occasionally bought all three on the shelf. You do not need a degree in mathematics to work out how many boxes I needed just to fill the stand, and to keep it full for the duration of the show needed many times this amount. I have often said that I did not do 'production' turning, but looking back, I wonder what else you would call turning 150 boxes to replace the stock sold at one show?

All this was in the days before the conservationists were saying that we should not use the beautiful exotic timbers, and that we were contributing to the destruction of the rainforests. My justification was, and still is, that if the timber had no value on the world market, the forests would just be felled and the land used for agriculture. By using them and giving them a high value there is the potential for harvesting a renewable crop, giving the countries exporting the timber a much-needed income. Fortunately, attitudes are becoming more enlightened: many suppliers advertise the fact that their timber is from renewable sources, and many exporting countries are now managing the supply sympathetically.

Four-stack box in rippled ash (no. 39)
h. 115mm (4$^{17}/_{32}$in), d. 65mm (2$^{9}/_{16}$in)

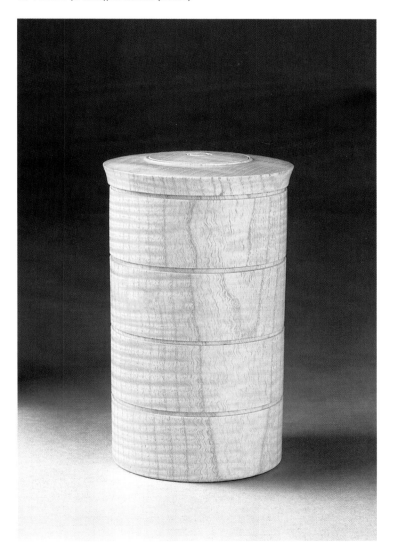

Common faults

Occasionally it all goes pear-shaped, sometimes literally. The faults that can occur in turned boxes are usually fairly basic:

1 The lid becomes a loose fit after a couple of days. This can be caused by the overheating of one part of the box when sanding. If the lid and base have differing moisture contents they will 'move' at different rates and cause this problem. Uneven thickness of lid and base could also be a cause.

2 The box distorts, so that the lid fits properly in only one position. This fault can arise from the timber being too wet when turned. Either rough-turn and allow to stabilize before turning to the final shape, or use dry wood to avoid this problem. Most boxes will eventually go slightly oval, but the lids should still fit.

3 Tiny cracks are seen in the top or base of the box, at right angles to the grain direction. These are heat checks due to overheating the wood when sanding with too fine a grit. Use the wax-lubricated sanding method to avoid creating too much heat.

4 The box splits wide open, as with the laburnum box shown here. This was caused by the wood being too wet (see 2 above), but it can also be caused by using the full width of the branch, including the pith – which is always a risky thing to do.

5 The box stays more or less round, but the lid keeps popping off. This is often caused by the spigot not being cut parallel, but it could also be due to 1, 2 or 4.

A Clam box in laburnum (see no. 35) which has split because of inadequate drying

6 Faults in the material itself, as the following little story demonstrates.

Recently I had an idea for a box shape, more or less like a doughnut, with chatterwork detail in the central recess. A short end of pink ivory which still had wax on the end grain took my eye, and this was duly mounted in the chuck and turned. I completed the lid in the usual way, and noticed that the colour was rather poor. However, when I started on the base I found the end grain deeply cracked under the wax – this had caused the colour to be affected – and although I did manage to complete the project it would never be saleable. I should know better than to pick up a piece of wood and start a project without checking it thoroughly first, but we all make mistakes – the main thing is to learn from them.

If you have trouble with a scrap-wood spigot being slightly undersize when jam-chucking, try wetting the spigot slightly. This will swell the wood and help it to grip. Another little trick I have learned over the years may also be of help when jam-chucking: a layer of beeswax melted onto the spigot will hold a piece more securely and allow heavier cuts.

Yew saucer (no. 20)
h. 82mm (3¹⁵/₆₄in), d. 168mm (6⁵/₈in)

Part II
50 Turned Boxes

Box 1

Simple box

Kingwood

h. 25mm ($^{63}/_{64}$in), d. 47mm ($1^{27}/_{32}$in)

Variations

- Make the lid flat or convex instead of concave. (This is the version shown below, and in the step-by-step photographs overleaf.)
- Round over the edge of the lid.
- Make the sides barrel-shaped.
- The inside could be curved instead of square-bottomed (you will need a round-ended scraper for this).
- The outside could be curved to give a smaller base.

All these variations can be tried without departing from the basic concept of a simple box that can be produced quickly.

At this stage I would advise against too much surface decoration, such as beads and coves, as they take extra time and add very little value to the project. Remember, if you wish to produce a 'quick' item, use the KIS technique: 'Keep It Simple'.

If you have never made a box before, this simple design is a good starting point. It provides good experience and practice in the techniques of making one part fit another, hollowing end grain, and parting off as cleanly as possible. Since this is the first and most basic of the 50 designs, each step is described in detail on the next two pages.

As there is little to commend this as a design, you now need to explore ways of improving this basic idea.

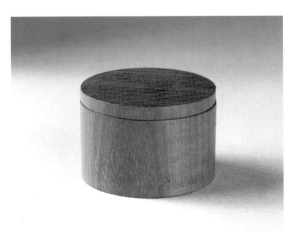

Flat-topped variation in purpleheart
h. 34mm ($1^{11}/_{32}$in), d. 48mm ($1^{7}/_{8}$ in)

Simple box

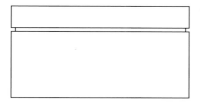

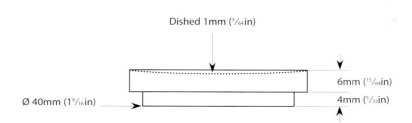

Dished 1mm ($^{3}/_{64}$in)

6mm ($^{15}/_{64}$in)

Ø 40mm (1$^{9}/_{16}$in)

4mm ($^{5}/_{32}$in)

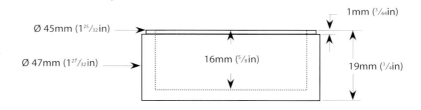

1mm ($^{3}/_{64}$in)

Ø 45mm (1$^{25}/_{32}$in)

Ø 47mm (1$^{27}/_{32}$in)

16mm ($^{5}/_{8}$in)

19mm ($^{3}/_{4}$in)

Box 1 | Simple box   49

Making a simple box

The tools I used are:

- roughing gouge
- 6mm (¼in) parting tool
- Superthin parting tool
- 10mm (³⁄₈in) spindle gouge
- 13mm (½in) square-ended scraper

The scraper is ground across the end and down the left-hand side. It is easier to control the scraper when the left-hand corner (as you look down at the face of the tool) is ground to just less than 90°, so that it is not cutting on the bottom and the side of the box at once. Rounding this same corner will give a softer line on the inside of the box.

1 Rough down, between centres, a piece of kingwood 50mm (2in) square by about 75mm (3in) long. With a parting tool, cut a spigot at one end to fit your chuck.

2 With the timber mounted in the chuck, true up the side and slightly hollow the end as shown in the drawing, using the 10mm spindle gouge.

3 Use the parting tool to cut a square-edged recess at the point where the lid divides from the base. The width of this recess will depend on what parting tools you have available – the 6mm (¼in) one is ideal for this. You can now sand, seal and polish the top and sides.

4 With your narrowest parting tool, part off the lid, leaving a fraction of the spigot showing on the base. Make your cut as clean as possible on the underside of the lid.

5 Hollow the base using the spindle gouge. Drill into the centre with the flute of the gouge facing away from you, then, with the tool horizontal and the flute towards you, cut outwards until you almost reach the edge of the small spigot left when the lid was parted off. Repeat until the final depth is reached.

A 50mm (2in) square of timber (purpleheart in this case) is mounted between centres and converted to a cylinder using the roughing gouge

Having formed a spigot on the end, remount the work in a chuck (this is the Craft Supplies chuck), part off a suitable length and true up the end and side using the 10mm (³⁄₈in) spindle gouge

Use the 6mm (¼in) parting tool to make a square recess which will form the spigot to locate the lid

The outside sanded, sealed and waxed

After parting off the lid, leaving a tiny part of the spigot intact, the base can be hollowed, by first drilling into the centre with the spindle gouge ...

6 Using the square-ended scraper, refine the inside, taking a series of fine cuts down the inside wall until you reach the diameter of the spigot. Take special care across the bottom: make sure that the scraper is cutting just above centre and the handle is always higher than the blade.

...then cutting outwards to remove the bulk of the material

7 This is the point at which the fit of the lid is determined. The less material removed, the more snugly it will fit. For this type of box, where the lid is solid and the base is hollowed, there is a tendency for the two parts to move at different rates; for this reason I prefer to make the lid an easy fit. At this stage a small cut can be made, creating a tiny rabbet or square groove at the point where the lid meets the base. This I call the *sight line*; it provides a visual break, emphasizing the proportion of lid to base, and will also disguise any small mismatch caused by the box warping slightly.

Refining the inside with the larger square-ended scraper; carefully cut up to the spigot mark until the lid fits

8 Sand and finish the inside of the box, and then part off, making sure that the underside is slightly hollow, so that it sits on the outer edge and is not inclined to wobble. Once again, if the underside is parted off cleanly, it will need minimal work to complete.

9 The box is now almost finished; all that may be needed is a little hand-sanding on the underside of the lid and across the bottom. If you have several boxes to do, a sanding pad can be put in the Jacobs chuck, fitted into the headstock, and the surfaces run over this, before sealing and polishing using one of the methods described on pages 40–2.

The inside sanded, sealed and waxed

Parting off with the Superthin parting tool; leave the underside slightly hollow for stability

Box 1 | Simple box   51

Box 2

Chinese hat box

Rio rosewood

h. 57mm (2¼in), d. 48mm (1⅞in)

This box follows the same basic format as the previous one, as the lid is just parted off without being hollowed. However, this time each surface is curved, making a much more interesting shape. Notice that the curves tighten towards the top and are not arcs of a circle.

The curve on the top of the lid starts off at right angles to the axis, which avoids making the lid too thick and heavy.

Once again, a tiny piece of the spigot is left on the top of the base to leave a guide for the diameter of the hole. The inside of the base can then be refined using the undercutting scraper. The outside shape is also a curve that tightens: the widest point is about a third down from the lip, after which it sweeps in towards the base. Try to make the base look as if it is joining up with the other side – that is, imagine that the box has a round bottom and the tiny foot is just a ring to lift it from the supporting surface. The foot itself is cut with the 3mm (⅛in) parting tool and parted off after finishing.

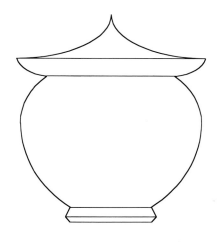

Chinese hat box

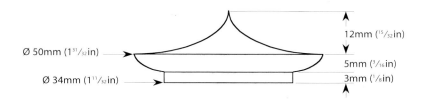

Ø 50mm (1³¹/₃₂in)

Ø 34mm (1¹¹/₃₂in)

12mm (¹⁵/₃₂in)

5mm (³/₁₆in)

3mm (¹/₈in)

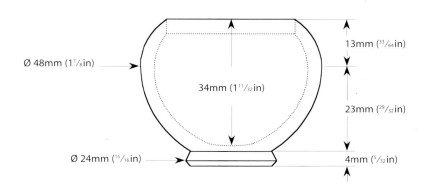

Ø 48mm (1⁷/₈in)

34mm (1¹¹/₃₂in)

Ø 24mm (¹⁵/₁₆in)

13mm (³³/₆₄in)

23mm (²⁹/₃₂in)

4mm (⁵/₃₂in)

Box 2 | Chinese hat box   53

Box 3

Onion-top box

Budgieroo

h. 94mm (3⁴⁵/₆₄in), d. 50mm (1³¹/₃₂in)

The Onion-top box evolved from the Chinese hat as I sought to make it more elegant by extending the lid upwards and adding a rather Oriental-looking, onion-shaped finial.

Making the box is approached in a similar manner to the previous one: cut the basic shape of the bottom of the box, form the spigot with the 6mm (¹/₄in) parting tool and then adjust the height of the top to give a balanced effect. The long curve leading up to the onion-shaped top is a critical part of this design: too thick and it will seem clumsy, too thin and it may seem fragile. Again the curve is one that tightens as it sweeps upwards, the narrowest part being about one third down from the point. The stem and the onion shape are all formed with the long-bevelled 10mm (³/₈in) spindle gouge. Once the top is sealed and polished, the lid can be parted from the base.

This time the base needs a little shelf for the top to sit in. This is cut with the 6mm (¹/₄in) square-ended scraper, again using as a guide the tiny bit of spigot that has been left on the top of the base. After cutting this, check that the lid fits before hollowing and refining the base, using the undercut scraper as before.

After polishing and finishing the inside of the base, the outside can be shaped, making sure that the curve flows into the shape of the lid. Any change in direction here will spoil the whole effect. The foot is once again cut with the 3mm (¹/₈in) parting tool and, after polishing, the base can be parted off.

Variations

- Replace the onion shape with a pointed or spear-shaped top (photo: page 25).
- A hollow, flared top gives a more vase-like appearance.

Flared-top variation in Mexican rosewood
h. 84mm (3⁵/₁₆ in), d. 47mm (1²⁷/₃₂ in)

Onion-top box

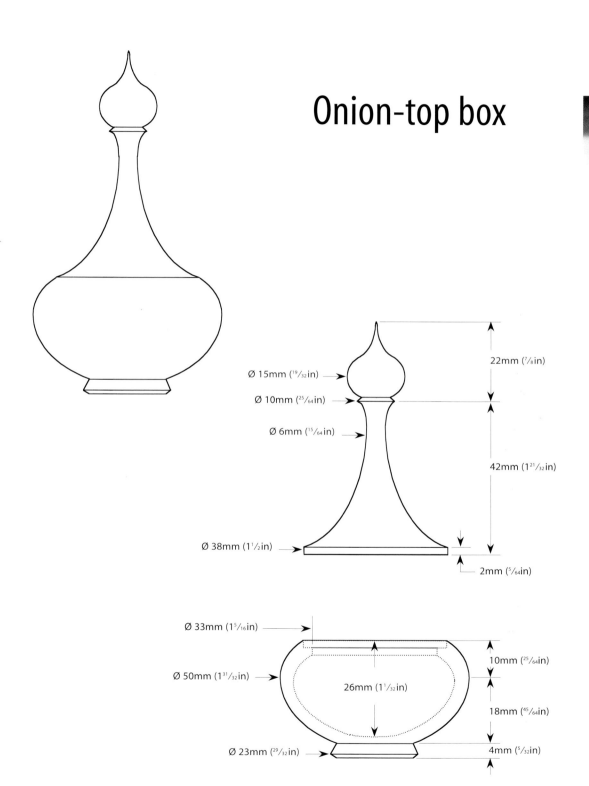

Ø 15mm ($^{19}/_{32}$in)

Ø 10mm ($^{25}/_{64}$in)

Ø 6mm ($^{15}/_{64}$in)

22mm ($^{7}/_{8}$in)

42mm ($1^{21}/_{32}$in)

Ø 38mm ($1^{1}/_{2}$in)

2mm ($^{5}/_{64}$in)

Ø 33mm ($1^{5}/_{16}$in)

Ø 50mm ($1^{31}/_{32}$in)

26mm ($1^{1}/_{32}$in)

10mm ($^{25}/_{64}$in)

18mm ($^{45}/_{64}$in)

Ø 23mm ($^{29}/_{32}$in)

4mm ($^{5}/_{32}$in)

Box 3 | Onion-top box   55

Box 4

Finial box

Pernambuco

h. 92mm (3⁵/₈ in), d. 49mm (1¹⁵/₁₆ in)

This was another of my 'craft-fair' boxes, and definitely the most popular, especially with the ladies. Notice that the lid is exactly twice the height of the body of the box, which is much the same as the Onion-top and its variations. These proportions are not what one would expect, and the design only works because the lid is relatively delicate. This box has often been copied, but I have seen very few that looked balanced. It is very easy to make the top too thick, and the whole effect is ruined.

After roughing down and cutting a spigot, the piece is fitted into the chuck, and the basic curve of the base turned. It is best to leave it thicker at the bottom for the time being, otherwise vibration could be a problem during hollowing. The spigot on the lid portion can then be cut using the 6mm (¹/₄ in) parting tool. Following this, the top can be roughed out to a carrot shape using the 12mm (¹/₂ in) Continental gouge, which is ideal for this.

The finial is turned with a long-bevelled 10mm (³/₈ in) spindle gouge, starting at the top and working down to the base of the lid, cutting each element as cleanly as possible. In order to get the proportions correct it may be easier to cut the large ball first, then complete the top portion and, finally, the lower part of the lid. I can cut this clean enough to need only 400 grit when sanding, but then I have made hundreds of these boxes. If you find you need to use coarser grits, there is a risk of losing definition. After sanding, the top needs sealing and waxing before parting off from the base.

As with the previous boxes, a tiny portion of

the lid spigot left on the base acts as a marker for the hollowing, and gives the diameter for the shelf that the lid sits on. The 6mm (¹/₄ in) square scraper is used for the shelf, and the undercut scraper will complete the inside curve. Sand and polish the inside before refining the outside shape using the 10mm (³/₈ in) gouge, and cut the foot with the 3mm (¹/₈ in) parting tool. After sanding and waxing, part off, leaving the base slightly hollow.

Variation

- The base can be extended to make it more like a goblet with a finial lid.

Variation with extended base, in yew
h. 138mm (5⁷/₁₆ in), d. 45mm (1²⁵/₃₂ in)

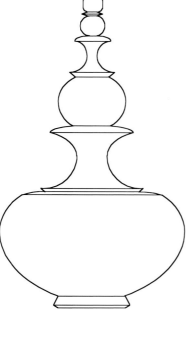

Finial box

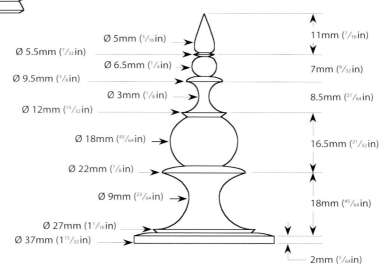

Ø 5mm ($^3/_{16}$ in) — 11mm ($^7/_{16}$ in)

Ø 5.5mm ($^7/_{32}$ in) —

Ø 6.5mm ($^1/_4$ in) — 7mm ($^9/_{32}$ in)

Ø 9.5mm ($^3/_8$ in) —

Ø 3mm ($^1/_8$ in) — 8.5mm ($^{21}/_{64}$ in)

Ø 12mm ($^{15}/_{32}$ in) —

Ø 18mm ($^{45}/_{64}$ in) → 16.5mm ($^{21}/_{32}$ in)

Ø 22mm ($^7/_8$ in) —

Ø 9mm ($^{23}/_{64}$ in) → 18mm ($^{45}/_{64}$ in)

Ø 27mm ($1^1/_{16}$ in) —

Ø 37mm ($1^{15}/_{32}$ in) → 2mm ($^5/_{64}$ in)

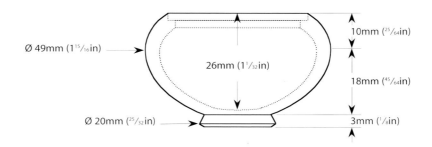

Ø 49mm ($1^{15}/_{16}$ in) → 10mm ($^{25}/_{64}$ in)

26mm ($1^1/_{32}$ in) 18mm ($^{45}/_{64}$ in)

Ø 20mm ($^{25}/_{32}$ in) → 3mm ($^1/_8$ in)

Box 4 | Finial box   57

Box 5

Easy box
Purpleheart
h. 52mm (2$^1/_{16}$in), d. 48mm (1$^7/_8$in)

This is another of my craft-fair boxes, although it was a little less popular than the preceding designs. Despite its name, it can be quite tricky to make.

The main features of this box are its square, straight-sided profile, the deeply coved, flaring lid, and the slightly hollowed top to the body of the box. The lid is set down into the top of the box, and it is this that can cause a few problems in the making. The top itself should present few difficulties apart from the deep cove, which may need a 6mm ($^1/_4$in) spindle gouge.

Start by turning the basic shape. It is necessary to leave a long spigot between lid and base – long enough to allow turning of the lid without fouling the base. The top edge needs to be kept crisp, so do not over-sand. Finish and part off the lid.

Being recessed below the top surface of the box, the recess for the lid needs a little care. Once this has been accomplished, the top surface of the base can be made to sweep outwards to give a shape which joins up with the curve of the lid; a round-ended scraper is useful here.

Hollowing is exactly the same as with previous boxes. This box will feel a little heavier than the previous ones because the outside shape does not match the inside.

Easy box

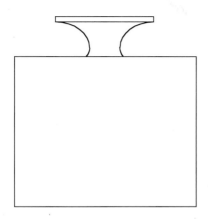

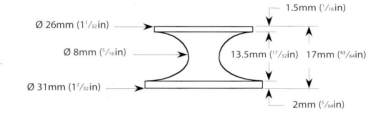

Ø 26mm (1¹/₃₂in)

Ø 8mm (⁵/₁₆in)

Ø 31mm (1⁷/₃₂in)

1.5mm (¹/₁₆in)

13.5mm (¹⁷/₃₂in)   17mm (⁴³/₆₄in)

2mm (⁵/₆₄in)

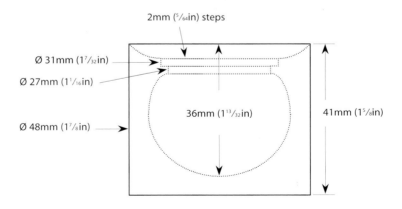

2mm (⁵/₆₄in) steps

Ø 31mm (1⁷/₃₂in)

Ø 27mm (1¹/₁₆in)

Ø 48mm (1⁷/₈in)

36mm (1¹³/₃₂in)

41mm (1⁵/₈in)

Box 5 | Easy box   59

Box 6

Spherical box
Leadwood
h. 57mm (2¹/₄in), d. 49mm (1¹⁵/₁₆in)

This is also a craft-fair-type box, although I didn't make very many because it developed towards the end of the period when I was doing fairs.

Construction is much the same as the previous box, but this time the basic shape is a sphere with a little flared handle on top. On this box a tight fit is advantageous during making,

enabling the curve of the base to be carried through into the lid to preserve the spherical form. If a looser lid is required, the fit can be eased later.

Rough out the basic shape and cut a spigot at the base of the lid with the 6mm (¹/₄in) parting tool. Once again, cut the recess to fit the lid. Hollowing is as before.

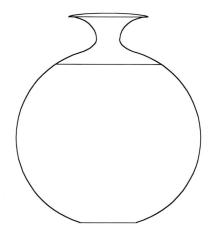

Spherical box

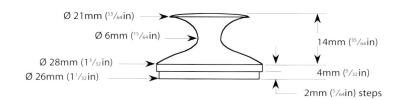

Ø 21mm ($^{53}/_{64}$in)

Ø 6mm ($^{15}/_{64}$in)

Ø 28mm (1$^3/_{32}$in)

Ø 26mm (1$^1/_{32}$in)

14mm ($^{35}/_{64}$in)

4mm ($^5/_{32}$in)

2mm ($^5/_{64}$in) steps

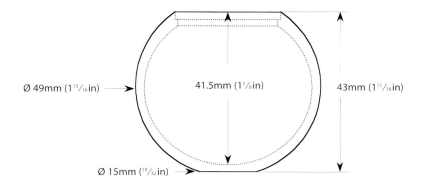

Ø 49mm (1$^{15}/_{16}$in)

41.5mm (1$^5/_8$in)

43mm (1$^{11}/_{16}$in)

Ø 15mm ($^{19}/_{32}$in)

Box 6 | Spherical box 61

Box 7

Vase box

Sonokeling

h. 70mm (2³⁄₄ in), d. 46mm (1¹³⁄₁₆ in)

This is the last of my craft-fair boxes. It was loosely modelled on a Grecian urn, showing that any pleasing shape can be converted into a box.

There is little to add to the instructions for previous boxes. However, it is critical for this one that the curve of the base blends into that of the top. The edges of the lid are slightly angled but should be kept crisp. Hollowing inside the base may present a few difficulties as it is slightly deeper than before, and hollowed through a smaller opening. As the tool is extended further over the rest, taking smaller cuts will give better control.

Sonokeling is easy to cut and an ideal choice for those new to box turning.

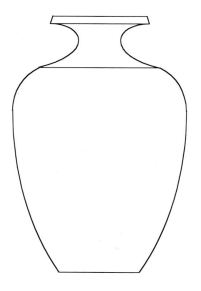

Vase box

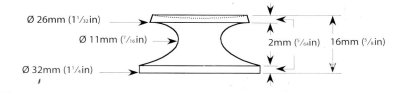

Ø 26mm (1¹/₃₂in)

Ø 11mm (⁷/₁₆in)

Ø 32mm (1¹/₄in)

2mm (⁵/₆₄in) 16mm (⁵/₈in)

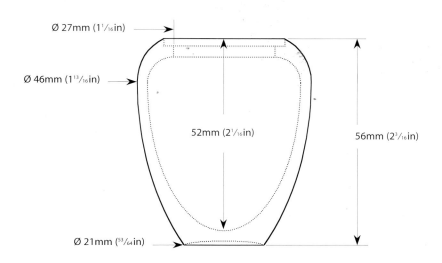

Ø 27mm (1¹/₁₆in)

Ø 46mm (1¹³/₁₆in)

52mm (2¹/₁₆in)

56mm (2³/₁₆in)

Ø 21mm (⁵³/₆₄in)

Box 7 | Vase box   63

Box 8

Beaded-lid box

Tulipwood

h. 52mm (2$^{1}/_{16}$ in), d. 47mm (1$^{27}/_{32}$ in)

This is the first of the boxes with a hollowed lid. It is more of a gallery item and likely to appeal to a box collector. As this box is a change of direction from previous ones, the technique is described in detail, step by step, on the next two pages.

This box involves jam-chucking, an essential skill which allows part of a box to be held on the lathe without marking it. This is achieved by cutting a spigot that fits the recess in a box lid or base; the recess is then literally jammed onto the spigot. Frequently a piece of softer, waste wood is used for the spigot, and this needs to be cut with a high degree of accuracy. It must be tight enough to drive the piece, but not so tight as to split it.

The making of this shallow-bodied variant is described and illustrated on pages 66–7.

Beaded-lid box

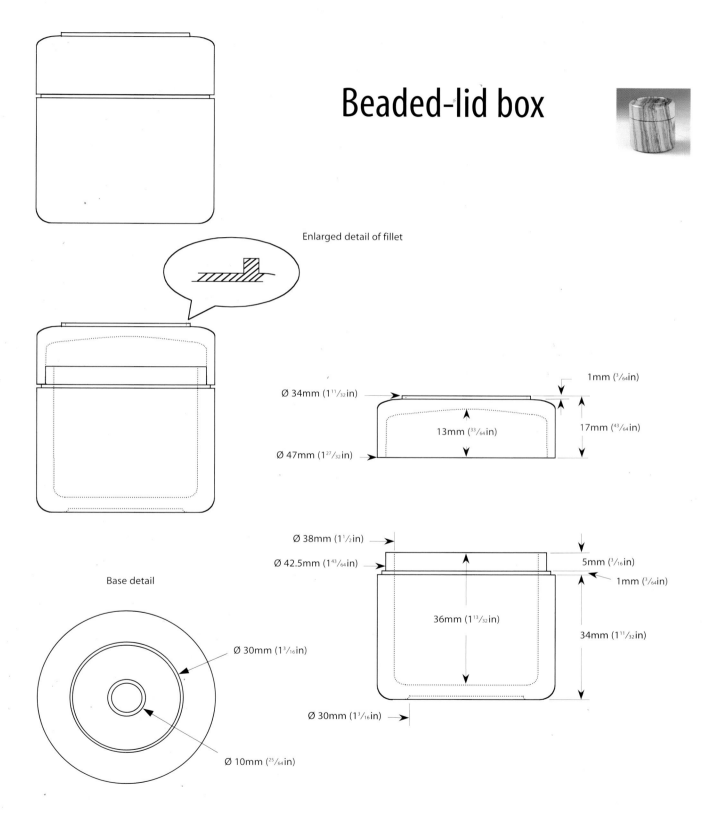

Enlarged detail of fillet

Ø 34mm (1¹¹⁄₃₂in)

1mm (³⁄₆₄in)

13mm (³³⁄₆₄in)

17mm (⁴³⁄₆₄in)

Ø 47mm (1²⁷⁄₃₂in)

Ø 38mm (1½in)

Ø 42.5mm (1⁴³⁄₆₄in)

5mm (³⁄₁₆in)

1mm (³⁄₆₄in)

36mm (1¹³⁄₃₂in)

34mm (1¹¹⁄₃₂in)

Ø 30mm (1³⁄₁₆in)

Base detail

Ø 30mm (1³⁄₁₆in)

Ø 10mm (²⁵⁄₆₄in)

Box 8 | Beaded-lid box   65

For a box with a snug-fitting lid, holding spigots are needed on each end

Hollowing the lid with the larger spindle gouge

Refining the inside of the lid with the large square-ended scraper

The inside of the lid sanded, sealed and waxed

Making a box with a hollowed lid

1 Rough down the timber, and cut a spigot on each end to fit the chuck.

2 Part off, leaving the portion for the lid still mounted in the chuck.

3 Hollow the lid using the drilling technique (see page 50) with the 10mm ($^3/_8$ in) spindle gouge.

4 Refine the inside shape using the square-ended scraper with a rounded corner. It is imperative that the two inner sides of the lid are parallel.

5 Sand and finish the inside of the lid.

6 With the base portion mounted in the chuck, cut a spigot 1.5mm ($^1/_{16}$ in) deep to match the inside of the lid.

7 Once the inside diameter of the lid has been marked on it, the box can be roughly hollowed using the 10mm ($^3/_8$ in) spindle gouge.

8 Now cut the spigot to its finished depth of 5mm ($^3/_{16}$ in), ensuring a tight fit for the lid. The lid is going to be jam-chucked onto the base of the box, so the fit needs to be tight enough to drive the lid without splitting it.

9 Measure the depth of the recess inside the lid; the overall height of the lid will be 3mm ($^1/_8$ in) more than this. With the lid mounted on the base, mark this height, plus an allowance of 3mm ($^1/_8$ in), and turn down to this level across the top of the box.

10 I have added an optional bead to the top of the lid by way of decoration. If you wish to follow this path you need to cut it with the little square-ended scraper, so

leaving a tiny square fillet (shown enlarged in the working drawing). The top surface inside this ring can be cut using the gouge, but it is easier to do this using light cuts with the little square-ended scraper. Once you are happy with the result, take the corners off the fillet. By the time you have sanded and polished the lid, this will be a round-edged bead.

11 While the lid is mounted on the base, you cannot determine the wall thickness. So, remove the lid and, with the 3mm (⅛in) parting tool, make a cut into the outside of the base down to your final wall thickness. At this point I also cut the sight line (the little square groove that shows where the box opens). Replace the lid and take the final finishing cuts to complete the outside shape.

12 Remove the lid and refine the inside of the base using the 13mm (½in) square-ended scraper with the rounded edge.

13 Sand, seal and polish the inside. The whole of the inside is now completed.

14 Measure the depth inside the body of the box and, leaving an allowance of 3mm (⅛in), make a cut for the underside of the base.

15 Replace the lid and finish all the outside.

16 Part off the base. Mount a piece of waste wood in the chuck and cut a spigot to fit the inside of the base. The base can now be jam-chucked onto this and the underside turned to a finish.

17 Check the fit of the lid and adjust the spigot if necessary. The box is now complete and ready for buffing or hand-polishing.

The base part roughly hollowed, with the spigot for the lid formed

The inside of the base part finished

Both parts are jam-chucked on waste wood in order to finish the outside

Box 8 | Beaded-lid box   67

Box 9

Zebrano box

Zebrano with holly knob

h. 73mm (2⁷/₈ in), d. 45mm (1²⁵/₃₂ in)

At first glance this is very similar to the Vase box (no. 7). However, this time the underside of the lid has been turned, and a contrasting wooden knob has been added. This box has a snug-fitting lid and takes longer to make. It therefore costs more, and so is really a gallery or collector's item.

A spigot is turned on each end of a roughed-out cylinder. After creating the overall basic shape, part off the piece for the lid, leaving it in the chuck. The underside of the lid can now be turned and finished. To take the knob, drill a 5mm (³/₁₆ in) hole using a Jacobs chuck in the tailstock.

The disc for the lid can now be parted off and set to one side for a while. Now, with the box base mounted in the chuck, the basic form is shaped. It is then hollowed and the recess cut to grip the lid securely.

With the lid fitted in place, the curve across the top of the lid can be blended in to the overall shape. At this stage the inside and the outside are finished, apart from the knob.

With a piece of holly mounted in the chuck (I would probably use the Axminster chuck with the engineering jaws for such a small piece), turn a 5mm (³/₁₆ in) spigot on the end. The neck of the knob can now be turned before gluing the box lid onto the spigot with superglue. Any excess spigot protruding through the lid can be trimmed off with a small gouge, and the underside polished.

Now the knob can be parted off and the lid reverse-chucked into a recess on a piece of waste wood. We are now in a position to complete the slight hollow in the top of the knob with a small spindle gouge before finishing.

The base can also be jam-chucked onto a spigot and the underside turned, sanded and polished. This requires a great deal of care, as the recess in the top of the box is very short, whilst the box is comparatively long and creates leverage. I used a 6mm (¹/₄ in) spindle gouge to reduce the danger of flipping the box base off the spigot.

Variations

- Replace the flat-topped knob with a spherical one.
- Make the knob in one piece with the lid (photo: page 27).

Variation with spherical knob in amazaque and holly h. 85mm (3¹¹/₃₂ in), d. 53mm (2³/₃₂ in)

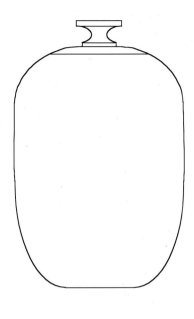

Zebrano box

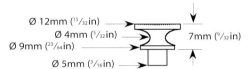

Ø 12mm ($^{15}/_{32}$in)

Ø 4mm ($^5/_{32}$in)

Ø 9mm ($^{23}/_{64}$in)

Ø 5mm ($^3/_{16}$in)

7mm ($^9/_{32}$in)

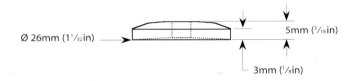

Ø 26mm ($1^1/_{32}$in)

5mm ($^3/_{16}$in)

3mm ($^1/_8$in)

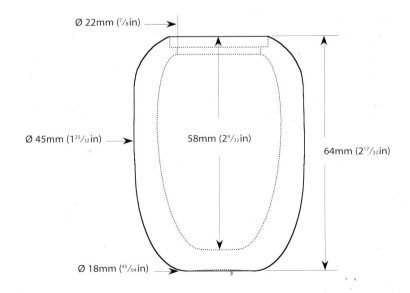

Ø 22mm ($^7/_8$in)

Ø 45mm ($1^{25}/_{32}$in)

58mm ($2^9/_{32}$in)

64mm ($2^{17}/_{32}$in)

Ø 18mm ($^{45}/_{64}$in)

Box 9 | Zebrano box 69

Box 10

Yew box
Yew branch
h. 66mm (2^{19}/$_{32}$ in), d. 74mm (2^{29}/$_{32}$ in)

I chose branch wood because of the lovely contrast that yew shows between the orange heartwood and the creamy sapwood. The shape, which I feel is quite critical in its proportions, brings out the best of these qualities.

As in most of these boxes with snug-fitting lids, the timber is roughed down and a spigot cut at each end. With the lid end mounted in the chuck the basic shape can be turned, leaving enough material between the lid and the base to form the spigot later. The piece for the lid is then parted off.

The inside of the lid can now be turned as before, once again making sure that the two sides are parallel. The underside is then ready for sanding and finishing. The flared side of the lid is turned before parting off, because it would be difficult to do this later when mounted on the box base.

With the box base mounted on the lathe, the spigot is cut and the inside roughly hollowed out, jam-fitting the lid to turn its top surface. With this completed, the lid is ready for sanding, sealing and finishing.

Now the full-bellied outside curve of the base needs to be refined using a spindle gouge, remembering not to make it too small at the foot. One thing to be wary of here is that the curve must meet the lid spigot at right angles; otherwise there would be a gap showing when the lid is fitted.

The base is now ready for the final hollowing out, which is done with the spindle gouge to remove the bulk of the material, followed by the little square scraper to cut the edges of the opening. Then the undercut scraper can be used to create a nice even wall thickness before sanding and sealing inside.

The next stage is to complete the outer curve down to the base, which is then sanded and sealed before parting off. Finally the box base is reverse-chucked onto a waste block to complete the underside.

Variation

● The lid can be made with a contrasting rim using the technique described on page 140; examples are shown below and on page 24.

Box in osage orange, with lid of chittam burl framed in karanda
h. 55mm (2^{5}/$_{32}$ in), d. 62mm (2^{7}/$_{16}$ in)

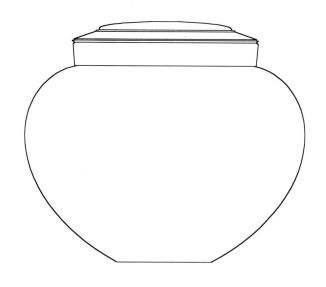

Yew box

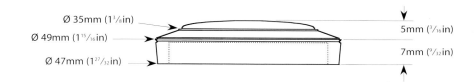

Ø 35mm (1³⁄₈in)

Ø 49mm (1¹⁵⁄₁₆in)

Ø 47mm (1²⁷⁄₃₂in)

5mm (³⁄₁₆in)

7mm (⁹⁄₃₂in)

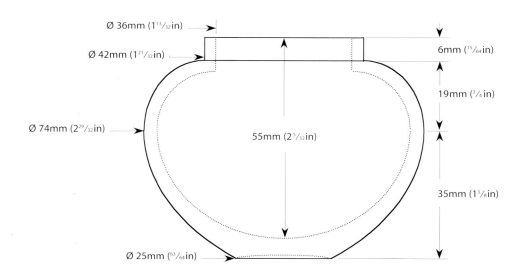

Ø 36mm (1¹³⁄₃₂in)

Ø 42mm (1²¹⁄₃₂in)

Ø 74mm (2²⁹⁄₃₂in)

55mm (2⁵⁄₃₂in)

6mm (¹⁵⁄₆₄in)

19mm (³⁄₄in)

35mm (1³⁄₈in)

Ø 25mm (⁶³⁄₆₄in)

Box 10 | Yew box   71

Box 11

Elegant box
Olivewood
h. 71mm (2^{25}/$_{32}$ in), d. 97mm (3^{13}/$_{16}$ in)

After making the Yew box, I had some misgivings about the shape, and decided to make a more refined version. This box, whilst retaining the same basic elements, has some features that lift it into another class. These are: the slightly flared shape of the lid, the tiny bead at the base, the ogee curve of the top, and a beaded ring around a concave centre. The beads are less than 1mm (1/$_{32}$ in) wide, and look delicate without being fussy. Anything larger would almost certainly have overpowered the basic shape. Precise working and sharp tools are essential for the beads, followed by minimal sanding to retain the crisp details.

The turning will present few problems other than the finishing. Olive is always an oily wood to work and awkward to sand, as the abrasive clogs almost immediately. Using creamed beeswax as a lubricant is the only way I have found to sand it successfully. However, the oil content, coupled with the absorbed wax, means that any shine never lasts long, and matts down to a dull sheen.

Variation

- A rounded edge to the lid is an alternative to the flared edge.

Variant with round-edged lid, in Indian rosewood
h. 78mm (3^{5}/$_{64}$ in), d. 95mm (3^{3}/$_{4}$ in)

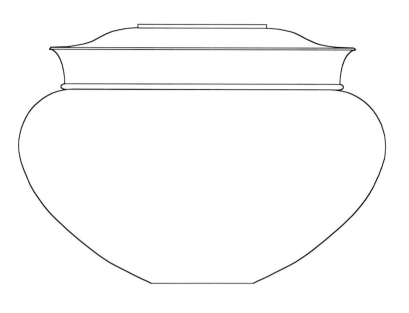

Elegant box

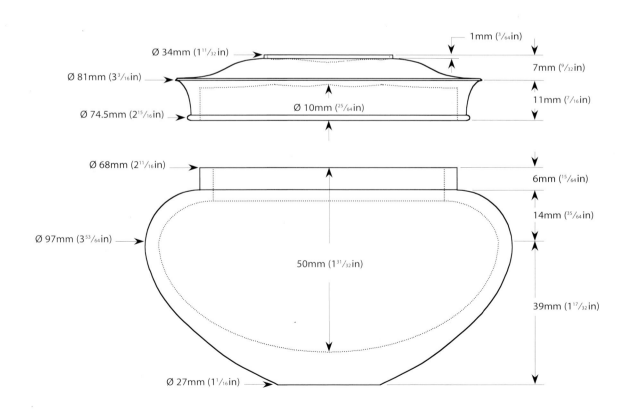

Ø 34mm (1¹¹/₃₂ in)

1mm (³/₆₄ in)

Ø 81mm (3³/₁₆ in)

7mm (⁹/₃₂ in)

Ø 10mm (²⁵/₆₄ in)

11mm (⁷/₁₆ in)

Ø 74.5mm (2¹⁵/₁₆ in)

Ø 68mm (2¹¹/₁₆ in)

6mm (¹⁵/₆₄ in)

14mm (³⁵/₆₄ in)

Ø 97mm (3⁵³/₆₄ in)

50mm (1³¹/₃₂ in)

39mm (1¹⁷/₃₂ in)

Ø 27mm (1¹/₁₆ in)

Box 11 | Elegant box 73

Box 12

Square-lidded box
Brazilian tulipwood

h. 61mm (2^{13}/$_{32}$ in), d. of box 45mm (1^{25}/$_{32}$ in),
w. of lid 47mm (1^{27}/$_{32}$ in)

This box could easily have been made using the 'craft-fair' format, but I chose the more difficult approach as being more appropriate to the high price of the timber. I think the appeal of this design is the contrast between the square-edged top and the brandy-goblet shape of the base.

This box needs a little more preparation than other shapes, because it starts with a length of wood which must be planed perfectly square. The area that will be the lid also needs sanding before turning commences, as it is easier to do at this point.

Whilst roughing down the basic cylinder it is essential to leave the square section for the lid undamaged. A spigot is cut on each end, and the square piece for the lid left in the chuck after parting off. The recess in the lid can be cut, sanded and polished, making sure that the underside of

the square rim is cut really cleanly. Cut as much of the top surface as possible at this stage before parting off, leaving enough material on top to complete the point on the lid.

If the lid is jam-chucked onto the base it is easy to catch the corners and knock the lid off the base. The corners are rotating like propeller blades and can give the turner a nasty rattle on the knuckles as well. I therefore find it easier to cut a spigot on a piece of waste wood, large enough to support the whole of the underside of the lid, and jam-chuck the lid onto this.

The box itself presents no problems. It is quite a simple shape and, as long as a nice brandy-glass curve is achieved, it should look well.

To avoid clumsiness it is essential to keep the lid as slim as possible without going through into the recess, as I did on one of my early attempts. (It is clear from the drawing how little spare material there is here.) Another point worth mentioning is that, with any box of this type, the inside of the box must have a parallel section at the opening, or there could be problems when reverse-chucking to finish the underside.

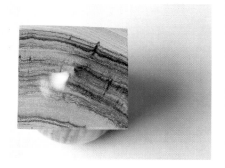

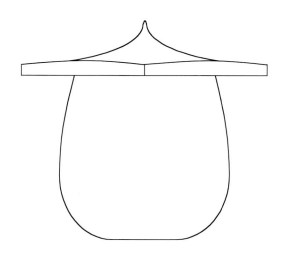

Square-lidded box

Lid is 47mm (1²⁷/₃₂in) square

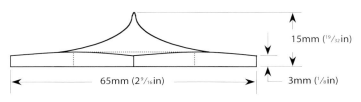

15mm (¹⁹/₃₂in)

65mm (2⁹/₁₆in)

3mm (¹/₈in)

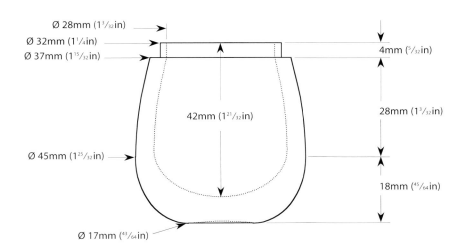

Ø 28mm (1³/₃₂in)

Ø 32mm (1¹/₄in)

Ø 37mm (1¹⁵/₃₂in)

4mm (⁵/₃₂in)

42mm (1²¹/₃₂in)

28mm (1³/₃₂in)

Ø 45mm (1²⁵/₃₂in)

18mm (⁴⁵/₆₄in)

Ø 17mm (⁴³/₆₄in)

Box 12 | Square-lidded box   75

Box 13

Pill box

Pink ivory

h. 54mm (2$\frac{1}{8}$ in), d. 49mm (1$\frac{15}{16}$ in)

This is one of my favourite designs, and one that breaks the 'rules' of proportion by having the lid and base almost equal in height; however, it looks OK to me. My original thought, when I started making this box, was to have the curved top dipping down into the centre to give a doughnut effect. I changed my mind partway through and

left the central flat area, decorating it with chatterwork, which is particularly effective on the fine grain of this pink ivory wood from Natal.

The making of this box follows the basic format for a snugly fitting lidded box. The points to watch are the radiused top and bottom corners, which need to match. The inside of the lid has been shaped leaving a small peak in the centre, purely to make it a little different. The overall effect of the finished box should be light and delicate.

Variations

Many variations are possible with this design. I enjoy fitting inserts of various contrasting woods into the tops of these boxes. Some have been done using the 'picture-frame' technique described on page 140, whilst others have chatterwork on the underside of the lid.

Several variations are illustrated: one in beautiful snakewood (page 26), one in ebony with a chittam burl insert, and two boxes with pink ivory inserts decorated with chatterwork (below and pages 5 and 25).

Variation in ebony and chittam burl
h. 27mm (1$\frac{1}{16}$in), d. 55mm (2$\frac{5}{32}$ in)

Variation in violet rosewood and pink ivory
h. 31mm (1$\frac{7}{32}$ in), d. 46mm (1$\frac{13}{16}$ in)

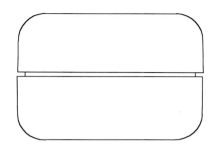

Pill box

Top of lid detail

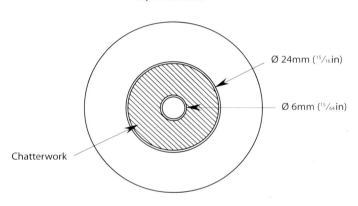

Ø 24mm ($^{15}/_{16}$in)

Ø 6mm ($^{15}/_{64}$in)

Chatterwork

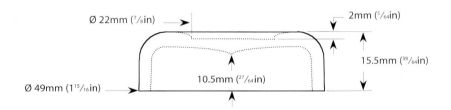

Ø 22mm ($^7/_8$in)

2mm ($^5/_{64}$in)

15.5mm ($^{39}/_{64}$in)

10.5mm ($^{27}/_{64}$in)

Ø 49mm (1$^{15}/_{16}$in)

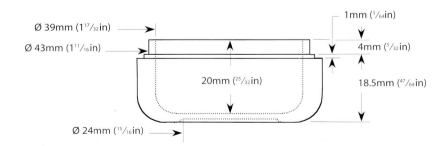

Ø 39mm (1$^{17}/_{32}$in)

Ø 43mm (1$^{11}/_{16}$in)

1mm ($^3/_{64}$in)

4mm ($^5/_{32}$in)

20mm ($^{25}/_{32}$in)

18.5mm ($^{47}/_{64}$in)

Ø 24mm ($^{15}/_{16}$in)

Box 13 | Pill box   77

Box 14

Teardrop box
Holly
h. 97mm (3¹³/₁₆ in), d. 51mm (2in)

The main appeal of this box, in my opinion, is the long S-curve of its profile. This long, clean line may present difficulties to beginners. Also, the proportion of lid to base is critical and may present more of a challenge than might be thought at first glance.

The holly had been cut into 75mm (3in) squares and stored for some time. A portion about 125mm (5in) long is mounted in the chuck, and a rough shape turned. A cut with the 6mm (¹/₄ in) parting tool is made along the line of the opening and the bottom section parted off, leaving the top in the chuck. The curved taper of the lid and the matching inside curve are now turned a little at a time, keeping the wall thickness as even as possible. The spigot for the body is cut, and the inside of the top can now be sanded and polished, and the lid finally parted off.

With the base now in the chuck, the recess has to be cut to match the spigot on the lid. This is always more difficult than the other way round. With the lid jam-fitted on the base it is now possible to complete the top and extend the curve down along the body of the box, creating this pleasing teardrop shape. After hollowing out the base, it can be reverse-chucked and the underside slightly hollowed as in the drawing.

Whilst turning this piece, I came across a small dead knot partway up the top, which has caused the box to warp slightly over time. I could have turned a replacement, but feel that this natural feature adds to the charm of the finished box.

This shape was inspired by a magazine article about a French company winning a design award for a bottle to contain spring water.

Due to the shape of this project the spigot needed to be on the lid, rather than the body of the box as is my usual practice. Otherwise the wall thickness would have been far too great. The lid needs to be an easy fit rather than a tight one, because the shape prevents it from being gripped tightly.

Teardrop box

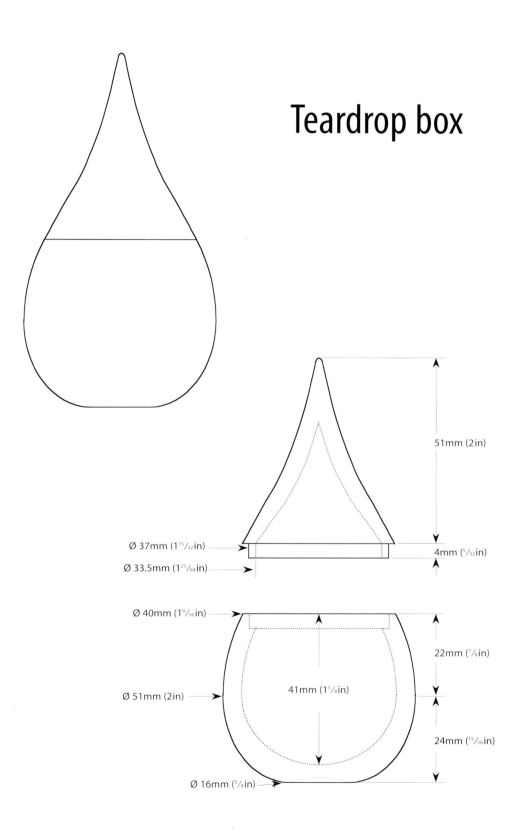

Ø 37mm (1¹⁵/₃₂in)

Ø 33.5mm (1²¹/₆₄in)

51mm (2in)

4mm (⁵/₃₂in)

Ø 40mm (1⁹/₁₆in)

Ø 51mm (2in)

41mm (1⁵/₈in)

22mm (⁷/₈in)

24mm (¹⁵/₁₆in)

Ø 16mm (⁵/₈in)

Box 14 | Teardrop box   79

Box 15

Ginger jar
Masur birch
h. 127mm (5 in), d. 66mm (2¹⁹/₃₂ in)

My choice of timber for this project had to have interesting end grain as well as being well figured down the side, and I think Masur birch is ideal. Although the grain patterns in these logs can be quite variable, this is a superb example, with the figure extending right to the centre and all round the log.

A start is made by roughing out the basic proportions, leaving the lid taller to allow material for the spigot. Then the lid can be turned first. The inside is hollowed with the gouge, followed by finishing cuts with a round-ended scraper. Birch is a soft timber and does not always cut as cleanly as the harder exotics. However, with sharp tools working with the grain – that is, from the centre out towards the rim – it does not present any problems. After cutting the outside of the lid, as far as the chuck allows, my wax-lubricated sanding technique (page 40) achieves an excellent surface for sealing and polishing.

The lid needs to be jam-chucked in order to turn the top. It is safer not to use the spigot on the box base for this, as there is a risk of damage to the soft wood. A longer spigot on a waste block is a sounder alternative.

The outer shape of the jar can now be started, leaving the bottom third unturned, for support, until the inside is completely hollowed out. Because of the depth of this project, and the fact that it is turned in end grain, I decided to use more drastic methods to hollow it than I usually do. I chose the Hamlet Big Brother hollowing tool, but there are many similar tools that will do the job just as well, so use what you have available. Once hollowed, the outside curve can be completed.

The box base is then ready for sanding and polishing inside and out. To clean up the underside, reverse-chuck onto a waste wood spigot. With long vessels it is advantageous to bring up the tail centre for support; the resulting central pip can be removed by hand later.

This design looks well in any highly figured wood, as the examples in laburnum and rippled ash (below and page 34) show. Page 18 shows another example in yew.

Ginger jar in laburnum
h. 110mm (4¹¹/₃₂ in), d. 75mm (2¹⁵/₁₆ in)

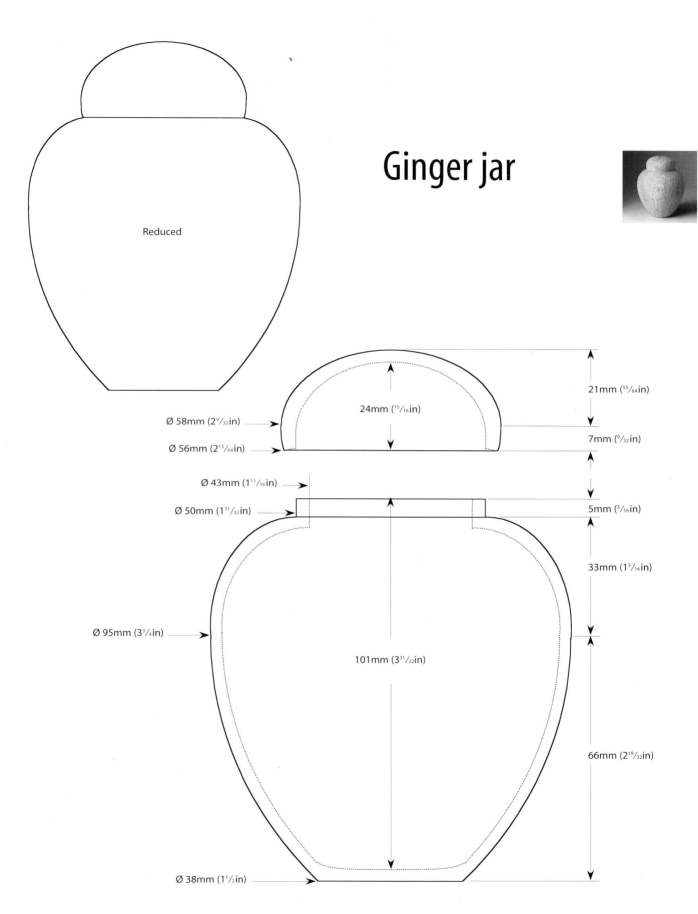

Ginger jar

Reduced

Ø 58mm (2⁹/₃₂in)

Ø 56mm (2¹³/₆₄in)

24mm (¹⁵/₁₆in)

21mm (⁵³/₆₄in)

7mm (⁹/₃₂in)

Ø 43mm (1¹¹/₁₆in)

Ø 50mm (1³¹/₃₂in)

5mm (³/₁₆in)

33mm (1⁵/₁₆in)

Ø 95mm (3³/₄in)

101mm (3³¹/₃₂in)

66mm (2¹⁹/₃₂in)

Ø 38mm (1¹/₂in)

Box 15 | Ginger jar   81

Box 16

Collector's box

Amarello (pequiá amarelo)

h. 57mm (2$\frac{1}{4}$ in), d. of box 60mm (2$\frac{3}{8}$ in),
d. of lid 64mm (2$\frac{17}{32}$ in)

This is the type of box that I have found to be popular with collectors of boxes, hence its name. Collectors seem to like the snug-fitting lid, the tiny beadwork and the overall machined appearance.

Incorporating raised beads, instead of cutting a square groove as a sight line, makes this box a little more of a challenge. I feel that the slightly flared sides of the lid complement the upward-sloping top very nicely.

Once again the underside of the lid is turned first; this time, because of the outside shape, the inner form can be domed to reduce weight.

The two tiny beads adjacent to the edges of the spigot are the tricky part of this project. One easy way to cut them is to mount the lid on the base, cut two little square beads using the 3mm ($\frac{1}{8}$in) parting tool and then take off the corners with the same tool; after sanding, the beads will be sufficiently rounded.

Turning the outside of the box part should not be too difficult. When turning the outside of the lid, the curve from the edge down to the bead may be a little tricky and needs good tool control. The line must flow into the base shape, but cutting has to halt cleanly at the bead.

The little step on the lid, about a third of the way in from the circumference, just breaks up an otherwise plain top.

Variations

There are numerous variations possible with this sort of design. The lid can be rounded, flat, or even slightly hollowed. The base can be straight, flared, curved in, or even have a round bottom, in which case it becomes a rocking box.

The example in cocobolo burr shown below is included as a variation on this design, even though at first glance they may seem to have little in common. By taking each small element of the design – top of lid, side of lid, base shape, decoration, timber – and changing one or more of these, we can create numerous alternatives to the original, while still keeping the basic concept of a lidded container.

Round-based variation in cocobolo burr
h. 38mm (1$\frac{1}{2}$ in), d. 67mm (2$\frac{21}{32}$ in)

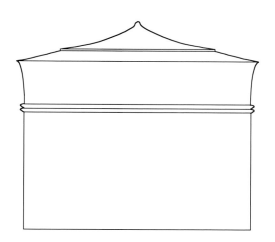

Collector's box

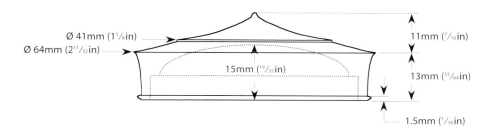

Ø 41mm (1⁵/₈in)

Ø 64mm (2¹⁷/₃₂in)

15mm (¹⁹/₃₂in)

11mm (⁷/₁₆in)

13mm (³³/₆₄in)

1.5mm (¹/₁₆in)

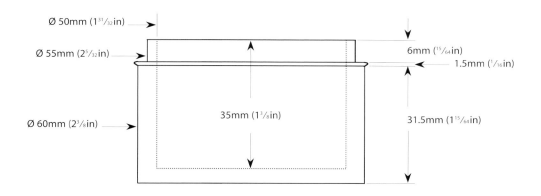

Ø 50mm (1³¹/₃₂in)

Ø 55mm (2⁵/₃₂in)

Ø 60mm (2³/₈in)

35mm (1³/₈in)

6mm (¹⁵/₆₄in)

1.5mm (¹/₁₆in)

31.5mm (1¹⁵/₆₄in)

Box 16 | Collector's box   83

Box 17

Mosque box

based on a design by Richard Raffan
Yew branch

h. 90.5mm (3^9/$_{16}$ in), d. of box 64mm (2^{17}/$_{32}$ in),
d. of lid 71mm (2^{51}/$_{64}$ in)

The design and the timber complement each other in this box, with the full curve of the dome showing off the white sapwood against the orange heart of the yew branch. The plainness of the straight-sided tower is broken by pippy features showing through the sapwood, and finished off by the bead where the dome and tower meet.

Selecting a length of yew branch with no heart checks is a feat in itself. If you are not fortunate enough to find one, then superglue, used at an early stage, will help.

With the lid section held in the chuck, cut the incurving section of the dome, the straight-sided part of the recess, and then remove the bulk of the inside with a gouge. The outside curve of the top can then be refined with the gouge, and the inside finished with the round-ended and undercut scrapers to achieve a nice wall thickness. After sanding, sealing and polishing the inside, the top can be parted off. The rest of the curve and the tiny finial are completed with the lid carefully jam-chucked onto the base spigot. Yew is a brittle wood and may split, so beware of using too much force when pushing the lid onto the spigot.

The box part is hollowed with a gouge, and the shape refined with a square-ended scraper, taking particular care with the end grain. All that remains is to form the tiny bead at the base of the spigot and the straight line of the outside, before parting off. Reverse-chucking onto a waste block is needed to complete the underside.

Variations

This design also suits other timbers. The two examples shown are in rippled bubinga and (page 40) superbly figured olive. The bubinga one is tiny, and both have a slightly flared base for variety.

Mosque box variation in bubinga
h. 58mm (2^9/$_{32}$ in), d. 49mm (1^{15}/$_{16}$ in)

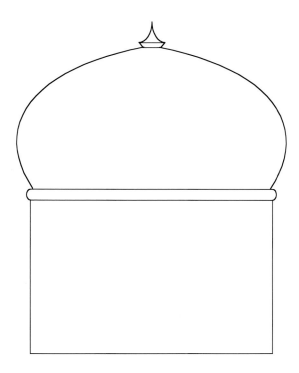

Mosque box

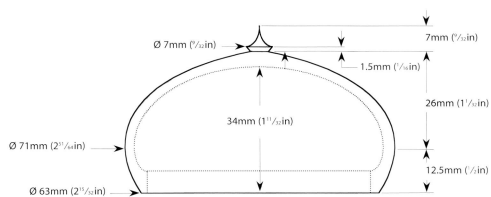

Ø 7mm ($^9/_{32}$in)

7mm ($^9/_{32}$in)

1.5mm ($^1/_{16}$in)

34mm ($1^{11}/_{32}$in)

26mm ($1^1/_{32}$in)

Ø 71mm ($2^{51}/_{64}$in)

Ø 63mm ($2^{15}/_{32}$in)

12.5mm ($^1/_2$in)

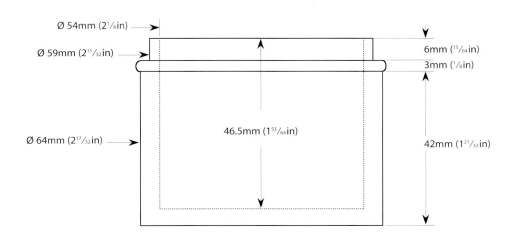

Ø 54mm ($2^1/_8$in)

Ø 59mm ($2^{11}/_{32}$in)

6mm ($^{15}/_{64}$in)

3mm ($^1/_8$in)

46.5mm ($1^{53}/_{64}$in)

Ø 64mm ($2^{17}/_{32}$in)

42mm ($1^{21}/_{32}$in)

Box 17 | Mosque box   85

Box 18

Egg box
Mahogany
h. 75mm (2¹⁵/₁₆ in), d. 46mm (1¹³/₁₆ in)

An egg has a beautiful shape, mainly because of the tightening curve. Turning an authentic egg shape is a good test of a turner's ability, but turning a box in this shape is an even greater test. Fortunately eggs vary a lot in shape, so there is a certain amount of leeway.

For this project I picked mahogany as it is a very easy turning wood. There are a great number of woods imported under the name of 'mahogany'; when selecting a piece for turning

I would recommend that you pick out the darkest and heaviest sample, as some of the lighter-coloured varieties are rather soft and stringy.

This box lies flat when finished; it does not stand up on its base. I suggest that the fatter end is treated as the lid of the box. This puts the join on the largest diameter, which is fortunately also about a third of the total length and gives good proportions to the finished item.

With the timber roughed round and spigots cut at either end, a piece can be parted off, leaving enough wood in the chuck for the lid. After removing the inside with a spindle gouge, the inner shape is completed with the round-ended scraper, taking care to leave the sides parallel at the opening. As the outside profile is turned, the wall thickness needs to be checked frequently and the inside shape adjusted if necessary. Before parting off, the inside of the lid has to be sanded, sealed and polished.

With the base part in the chuck, the spigot is cut to fit the inside of the lid, and then the lid is jam-fitted onto the base. Now the upper portion of the box can be completed. With the top still jammed on, the curve is extended down towards the pointed end. Before too much material is removed, the inside needs to be hollowed in the same way as for the lid. The final stage is to jam-chuck the box base on a piece of waste wood and complete the pointed end of the egg.

What looks to be a very easy project can take a little more care than might be thought at first glance.

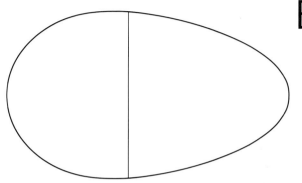

Egg box

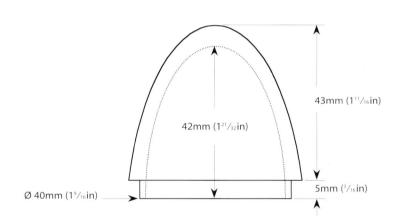

43mm (1¹¹/₁₆in)

42mm (1²¹/₃₂in)

5mm (³/₁₆in)

Ø 40mm (1⁹/₁₆in)

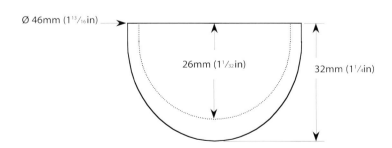

Ø 46mm (1¹³/₁₆in)

26mm (1¹/₃₂in)

32mm (1¹/₄in)

Box 18 | Egg box 87

Ball box

Sycamore

d. 56mm (2⁷/₃₂ in)

A spherical box looks as though it is easy to make, but looks can be deceptive. The easiest way of tackling it is to make templates. However, in an effort to create a perfect sphere, I prefer to go a different way.

The basic shaping and hollowing follows the methods used in the earlier projects, but this time careful measuring is essential: the length has to match the diameter.

With the nearly finished box assembled, it needs to be rotated through 90° – that is, with the join parallel to the lathe bed – and then turned again. To do this you will need to make a cup chuck to fit onto the revolving centre, and another to be held in the four-jaw chuck; the box is then held between the two (see the drawing below). The blurred outline of the rotating box is now turned away to leave a pretty good sphere. Sanding is also carried out whilst the box is held in the cup chucks; the position of the box must be changed several times during the process to ensure that the whole surface is adequately sanded.

When I made my first Ball box I turned the walls too thin, which caused the box to flex when held between the cup chucks. A harder, stronger timber, or thicker walls, would have eliminated the problem.

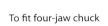

To fit four-jaw chuck

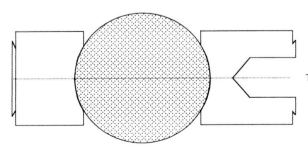

To fit tailstock revolving centre

Turning the Ball box using cup chucks

Ball box

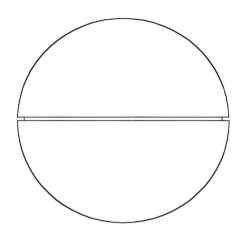

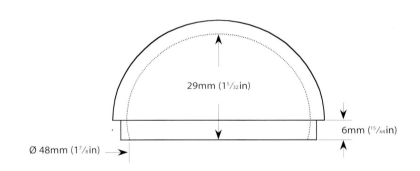

29mm (1⁵/₃₂in)

6mm (¹⁵/₆₄in)

Ø 48mm (1⁷/₈in)

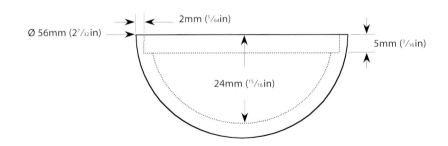

2mm (⁵/₆₄in)

Ø 56mm (2⁷/₃₂in)

5mm (³/₁₆in)

24mm (¹⁵/₁₆in)

Box 19 | Ball box   89

Box 20

Yew saucer

Yew

h. 82mm (3^{15}/$_{64}$ in), d. 168mm (6^{5}/$_{8}$ in)

This is a box I have made quite a lot in the past, when I had a good source of small yew logs about 150mm (6in) in diameter. The logs were planked into 50mm (2in) slabs; the body of the box was cut from a plank and was arranged to show sapwood evenly on either side. The lid was then made from an outer plank, and therefore showed more sapwood. The knob came from a small piece of branch wood. As I do not have the same supplies of timber these days, I have had to compromise and the box shown has sapwood only on one side.

As described above, the box is cut from side-grain wood, so turning can be started on a screw chuck in what will be the top of the main section. The lower part of the base can be shaped and a spigot cut where the foot will be. By holding the box on this spigot, the upper curve can be turned and the centre hollowed. Side grain is more difficult to hollow than end grain: scrapers will tend to produce 'tear-out' where they hit the end of the grain. This can be minimized by taking light cuts with a very sharp scraper. Reaching the widest part under the top surface could present some problems, but you cannot grind a special tool for each design, so you manage as well as you are able. The opening is fairly wide, so access is not restricted too much. Sanding is probably best done using wet sanding with the soft wax (see page 40) in order to avoid the heat-checking to which yew is very prone. To complete the base, the box can be held by its opening, with expanding jaws on the four-jaw chuck, or on a jam-fit chuck of scrap wood.

The lid should present few problems. It can be held on a screw chuck if the wood is thick enough, or glued onto a waste block. The underside is turned first, a spigot is cut to fit the base, then the lid is reverse-chucked into a recess in a scrap block, to complete the top. The lid should be sanded and polished at each stage. The knob is turned from a piece of branch wood and glued in place.

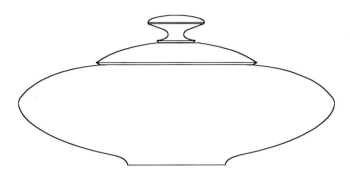

Yew saucer

Reproduced at half actual size

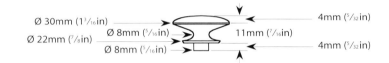

Ø 30mm (1³/₁₆in) ——
Ø 22mm (⁷/₈in) ——
    Ø 8mm (⁵/₁₆in) ——
    Ø 8mm (⁵/₁₆in) ——
—— 4mm (⁵/₃₂in)
11mm (⁷/₁₆in)
—— 4mm (⁵/₃₂in)

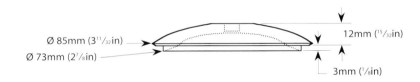

Ø 85mm (3¹¹/₃₂in) ——
Ø 73mm (2⁷/₈in) ——
12mm (¹⁵/₃₂in)
3mm (¹/₈in)

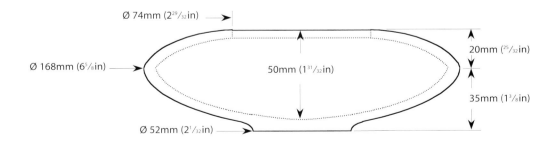

Ø 74mm (2²⁹/₃₂in) →
Ø 168mm (6⁵/₈in) →
50mm (1³¹/₃₂in)
20mm (²⁵/₃₂in)
35mm (1³/₈in)
Ø 52mm (2¹/₃₂in) →

Box 20 | Yew saucer 91

Box 21

Footed box

Eucalyptus burl

h. 70mm (2³⁄₄ in), d. 98mm (3⁵⁵⁄₆₄ in)

When I started turning this beautiful piece of burl, I intended making a small hollow form; however, small items rarely achieve a price that matches the time spent on them. With the piece already mounted on the screw chuck, I altered my plans and decided to make it into a box. Fortunately I had enough material to take a slice off the bottom for the lid, which is why it does not match perfectly – it would have been far better to cut it from the top surface.

Eucalyptus burl can twist and warp dramatically during drying, so this is one wood that needs rough-turning and stabilizing for some time. The main feature of this box is the continuous oval curve of the underside, lifted by the four feet.

Cutting a slice from the end of a bowl blank on the bandsaw can be very dangerous unless the wood is held in a vee-block, or some other kind of cradle. If you do not have this facility, then either glue the blank to a larger block and part off a slice, or saw it by hand.

The body can be fitted to a screw chuck and the outer curve turned, leaving a spigot (from which the feet will later be cut) for the chuck. The inside should be cut and scraped to a matching shape; eucalyptus burl will scrape extremely well with virtually no tear-out.

The thin slice for the top will probably have to be glued to a block while the underside is turned, making sure that it fits the hole in the base. Turn as much of the top shape as you can before removing it from the block and jam-fitting into the base or a waste block.

To make the feet, hold the body with the expanding jaws in the hole and convert the spigot into a ring, making sure that the area within the ring is curved to match the outside. Mark out the feet and cut away the waste – I used a Power File to blend in the curve of the base between the feet, but in the past I have used small rasps and abrasives to do the same job.

The knob can be made from ebony or any other contrasting timber and glued in.

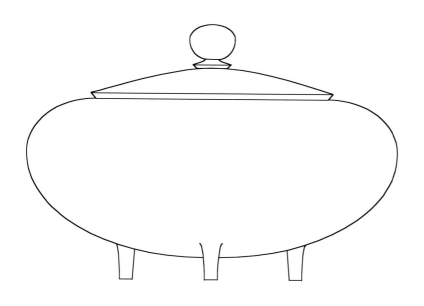

Footed box

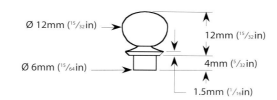

Ø 12mm ($^{15}/_{32}$in) →

Ø 6mm ($^{15}/_{64}$in) →

12mm ($^{15}/_{32}$in)

4mm ($^{5}/_{32}$in)

1.5mm ($^{1}/_{16}$in)

Ø 64mm (2$^{17}/_{32}$in) →

Ø 49mm (1$^{15}/_{16}$in) →

8mm ($^{5}/_{16}$in)

4mm ($^{5}/_{32}$in)

1.5mm ($^{1}/_{16}$in)

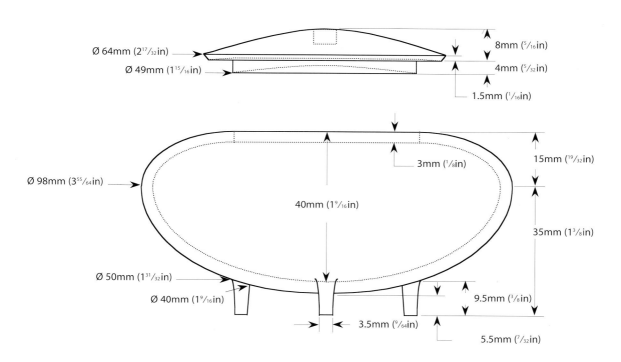

3mm ($^{1}/_{8}$in)

15mm ($^{19}/_{32}$in)

Ø 98mm (3$^{55}/_{64}$in) →

40mm (1$^{9}/_{16}$in)

35mm (1$^{3}/_{8}$in)

Ø 50mm (1$^{31}/_{32}$in) →

Ø 40mm (1$^{9}/_{16}$in) →

9.5mm ($^{3}/_{8}$in)

3.5mm ($^{9}/_{64}$in)

5.5mm ($^{7}/_{32}$in)

Box 21 | Footed box   93

Box 22

Mushroom box
Boxwood
h. 54mm (2$\frac{1}{8}$ in), d. of lid 58mm (2$\frac{9}{32}$ in)

The base piece can then be held in the chuck and roughly hollowed. Cut the spigot to be a tight fit in the lid, and mount the lid. Complete the top curve, sand, and finish the lid completely.

The outside profile of the body of the box can now be cut, and the inside shaped with the round-cornered scraper. After sanding and polishing, the body can be re-chucked on a waste block and the underside completed.

This is a nice little project that needs a little care with the proportions, and smooth curves, to set it off. As an alternative, I also turned a natural-edged mushroom box from a similar piece of boxwood, as shown below.

Mushrooms and toadstools come in all shapes and sizes, so there is a fair amount of leeway in this design. This box was made from spalted boxwood, as the colour seemed very appropriate for this project.

With the lid section mounted in the chuck, the rolled edge can be turned and blended into the underside chamfer. The recess then needs to be hollowed with a gouge, and the curved inside top cut with a round-ended scraper. The square-ended scraper is then used to cut the sides of the recess, making sure that these are parallel. After sanding and polishing the underside, turn as much of the top curve as possible with a gouge, then part it off, ensuring that there is enough material to complete the curve.

Natural-edged variation in boxwood
h. 57mm (2$\frac{1}{4}$ in), d. 97mm (3$\frac{13}{16}$ in)

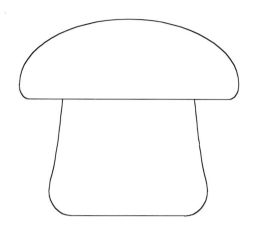

Mushroom box

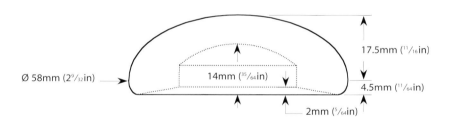

Ø 58mm (2⁹/₃₂in)

14mm ($^{35}/_{64}$in)

17.5mm ($^{11}/_{16}$in)

4.5mm ($^{11}/_{64}$in)

2mm ($^{5}/_{64}$in)

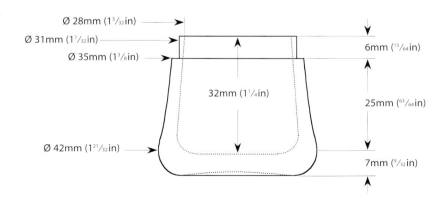

Ø 28mm (1³/₃₂in)

Ø 31mm (1⁷/₃₂in)

Ø 35mm (1³/₈in)

Ø 42mm (1²¹/₃₂in)

32mm (1¹/₄in)

6mm ($^{15}/_{64}$in)

25mm ($^{63}/_{64}$in)

7mm ($^{9}/_{32}$in)

Box 22 | Mushroom box   95

Box 23

Apple box
Acacia burl
h. 108mm (4$\frac{1}{4}$ in), d. 88mm (3$\frac{15}{32}$ in)

plenty of 'meat' at the chuck end to support the inside scraping cuts. Don't forget to allow a little extra thickness in the centre to support the stem; the whole effect would be spoiled if the hole went right through.

The base can be turned in a similar manner, then both lid and base need to be reverse-chucked to complete the ends.

The stem can be turned from a small piece of ebony turned into a curved taper, ending in the same diameter as the hole. This needs to be cut off at an angle and finished on a belt sander before being glued into the hole.

Variations

Several other kinds of fruit may lend themselves to similar treatment – pears or gourds, for example.

This box is turned from one of my favourite English woods, which is acacia burl, or more correctly *Robinia pseudoacacia*. Its beautiful tight grain makes it very easy to turn – even when using a scraper there is seldom any tear-out – and its colour makes it an ideal wood for the subject.

With a piece of wood this size, rough-turning is essential. I cut spigots on each part and roughed out the general shape, then left it to stabilize for about six weeks before attempting the finishing process.

When turning the top half of the box, develop the outside curve for a short distance, then cut the inside to match. Working in stages like this leaves

Pear box in acacia
h. 140mm (5$\frac{1}{2}$ in), d. 90mm (3$\frac{35}{64}$ in)

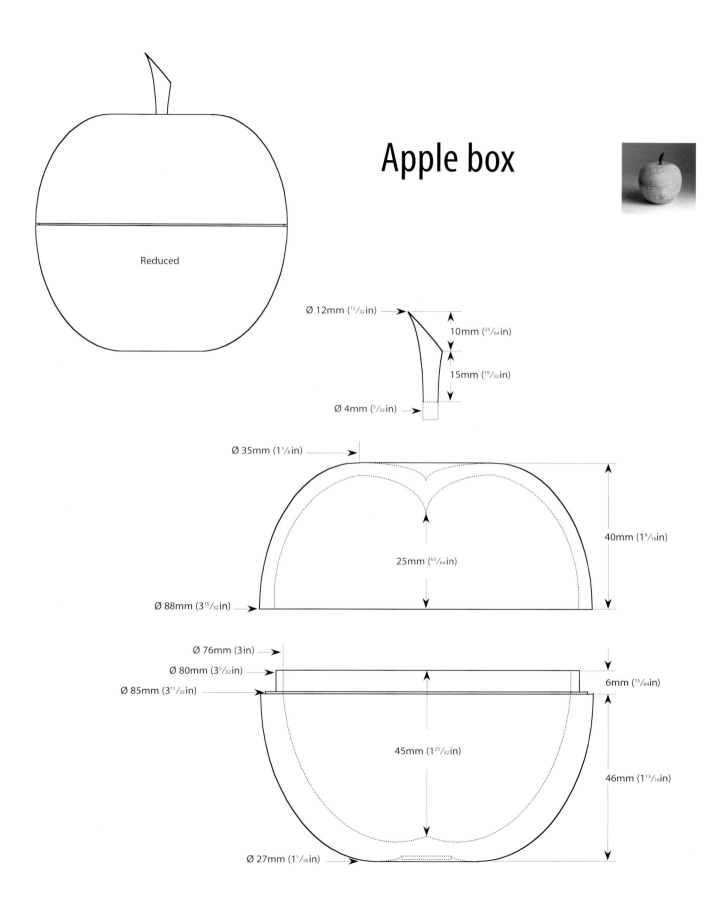

Apple box

Reduced

Ø 12mm ($^{15}/_{32}$ in)

10mm ($^{25}/_{64}$ in)

15mm ($^{19}/_{32}$ in)

Ø 4mm ($^5/_{32}$ in)

Ø 35mm (1$^3/_8$ in)

40mm (1$^9/_{16}$ in)

25mm ($^{63}/_{64}$ in)

Ø 88mm (3$^{15}/_{32}$ in)

Ø 76mm (3 in)

Ø 80mm (3$^5/_{32}$ in)

Ø 85mm (3$^{11}/_{32}$ in)

6mm ($^{15}/_{64}$ in)

45mm (1$^{25}/_{32}$ in)

46mm (1$^{13}/_{16}$ in)

Ø 27mm (1$^1/_{16}$ in)

Box 23 | Apple box   97

Box 24

Saturn box
Putumuju
h. 50mm (1³¹/₃₂ in), d. of ring 75mm (2⁶¹/₆₄ in)

Hans Weissflog of Germany (some of whose work can be seen on pages 170–3) turns Saturn boxes, but he cuts through the rim at an angle from both sides, allowing it to rotate yet still be captive. In deference to him I have left mine with an attached solid rim.

This is one of the few projects that require templates to be used. I cut mine from a piece of laminate. If this is held on a wooden faceplate using double-sided tape, the male inside profile and the female outer profile can be cut cleanly with the Superthin parting tool. The female pattern can then be cut in half and a portion removed to allow for half the thickness of the rim.

Turning a sphere is not easy, and any deviation from the perfect line will show; that is why I recommend using templates. The rim prevents the use of the cup-chucking technique used with the Ball box (no. 19). The timber should be chosen for easy cutting, with reasonable strength across the grain, because the disc is just thin end grain.

Begin by chucking the piece in the normal manner, and parting off enough for the top hemisphere. The inside can then be hollowed using the template as a guide; note that the inner top is not a perfect hemisphere, as the sides need to be parallel to mate with the spigot. Turn the outside to as near the final shape as possible before parting off. Reverse-chuck onto a waste block and complete the outer profile according to the template.

After chucking up the lower part, cut the spigot, hollow the inside, turn away the bulk of material below the disc and then reverse-chuck yet again to complete the lower portion. Once again the sanding, sealing and polishing have to be completed at each stage before moving on to the next. This box also needs an easy-fitting spigot; otherwise it would be difficult to open.

This is a very satisfying box to make, as it needs a lot of careful cutting and attention to detail to create the perfect shape.

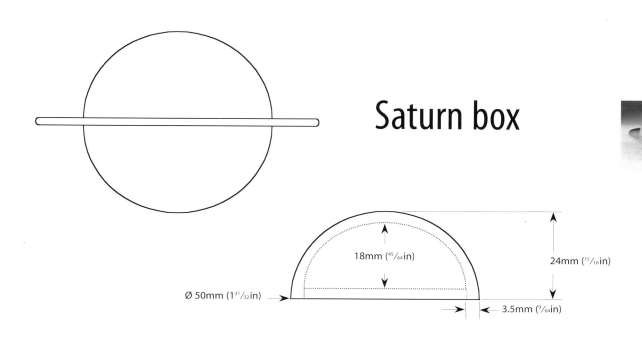

Saturn box

18mm ($^{45}/_{64}$in)

24mm ($^{15}/_{16}$in)

Ø 50mm (1$^{31}/_{32}$in)

3.5mm ($^{9}/_{64}$in)

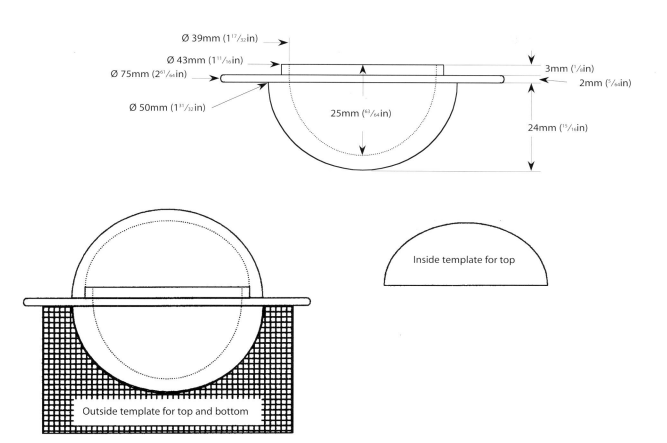

Ø 39mm (1$^{17}/_{32}$in)

Ø 43mm (1$^{11}/_{16}$in)

Ø 75mm (2$^{61}/_{64}$in)

Ø 50mm (1$^{31}/_{32}$in)

3mm ($^{1}/_{8}$in)

2mm ($^{5}/_{64}$in)

25mm ($^{63}/_{64}$in)

24mm ($^{15}/_{16}$in)

Inside template for top

Outside template for top and bottom

Box 24 | Saturn box 99

Box 25

Japanese lantern box

African teak

h. 67mm (2⅝ in), d. of lid 49mm (1¹⁵⁄₁₆ in),
d. of base 54mm (2⅛ in)

I have always been fascinated by Bonsai trees and Japanese gardens, so a box in the shape of a Japanese lantern really appealed to me. Most of these lanterns are square, but it did not take too much imagination to convert one into this round shape. For those of you who have some interest in Japanese garden design, this project is based loosely on an *Oki-gata* lantern.

African teak is not the nicest timber to work with, but it is very hard and strong. The wood needs to be strong because the first step is to check it for square, mark it out and drill the holes through the base. Any discrepancy in either squareness or drilling will mean odd-sized legs, with little hope of altering them.

The timber is then roughed round and spigots cut at either end. With the piece for the lid mounted in the chuck, the rest is parted off. The underside of the lid can be completed with round-ended and square-ended scrapers, sanded and polished. The basic taper of the top surface is completed, and the top detached from the chuck. The base part now needs to be chucked and the spigot cut to fit the roof. With the lid jammed on, the steps in the roof are cut, which adds a little relief to an otherwise uninteresting grain pattern.

With the top complete, the box part can now be attended to. Because of the two holes drilled through the timber, the wood will be quite weak, and the spigot for the lid is also a long way out from the chuck. This means that the hollowing process needs very small cuts from a square-ended scraper, after the initial opening up with a small gouge. Then the outside shape and the small bead are completed. Finally, the outside curve of the legs can be cut. After sanding and polishing, the legs need to be cut through with a fine-toothed saw, after first marking with a cut from the skew.

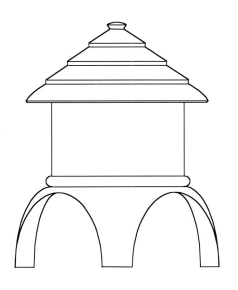

Japanese lantern box

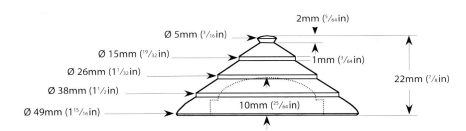

2mm (⁵/₆₄ in)

Ø 5mm (³/₁₆ in)

Ø 15mm (¹⁹/₃₂ in)

1mm (³/₆₄ in)

Ø 26mm (1¹/₃₂ in)

Ø 38mm (1¹/₂ in)

22mm (⁷/₈ in)

Ø 49mm (1¹⁵/₁₆ in)

10mm (²⁵/₆₄ in)

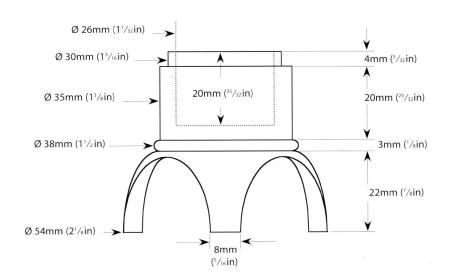

Ø 26mm (1¹/₃₂ in)

Ø 30mm (1³/₁₆ in)

4mm (⁵/₃₂ in)

Ø 35mm (1³/₈ in)

20mm (³⁵/₃₂ in)

20mm (²⁵/₃₂ in)

Ø 38mm (1¹/₂ in)

3mm (¹/₈ in)

22mm (⁷/₈ in)

Ø 54mm (2¹/₈ in)

8mm
(⁵/₁₆ in)

Box 25 | Japanese lantern box   101

Box 26

Pagoda box
Olive ash
h. 103mm (4$^{1}/_{16}$in), w. of lid and base 72mm (2$^{53}/_{64}$in)

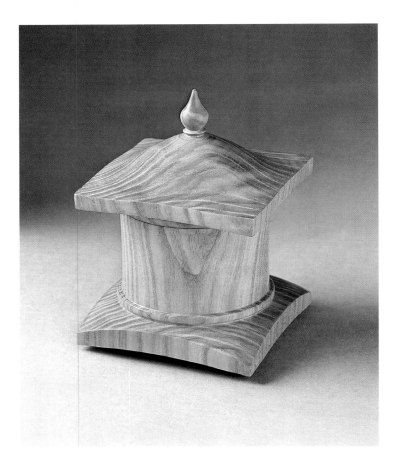

This second lantern is based on an *Ikekomi-gata* design, but could be converted to a *Tachi-gata* lantern by adding a tall pedestal. I did contemplate this, then decided that it would be too unstable perched on a tall column.

The first consideration with this project is to ensure that the timber is perfectly square. Once this is verified it can be accurately mounted between centres to cut spigots on either end, and to make the central part round. After parting off a portion for the lid, the recess is cut and the bead under the 'roof' can be formed. A clean cut with the long-bevelled 10mm ($^{3}/_{8}$in) spindle gouge completes the underside. Bearing in mind that there will be very little support once the top is held on a jam chuck, I turn as much of the top curve as possible before parting off. This leaves just the tiny finial and the finishing to do when reversed and jam-chucked.

Although it makes the top more difficult to turn, I feel that putting the bead on the underside of the lid gives me a little more depth to play with when cutting the recess. Otherwise, it would probably be easier to turn if the bead were at the top of the box part instead.

Turning the base presents few problems, other than achieving a clean cut on the square section, without chipping the edges. To cut the square section as cleanly as possible, I suggest running the lathe at a high speed, taking very small cuts, and just skimming the surface of the wood with the bevel.

When reversing the base on a jam chuck, I cut a recess in the centre so that if necessary a hollowed pedestal could be added, thereby creating a double box.

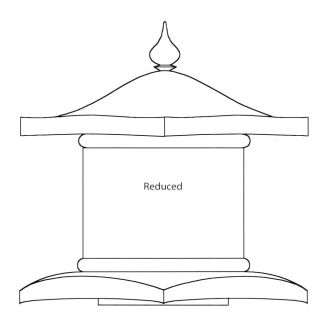

Reduced

Pagoda box

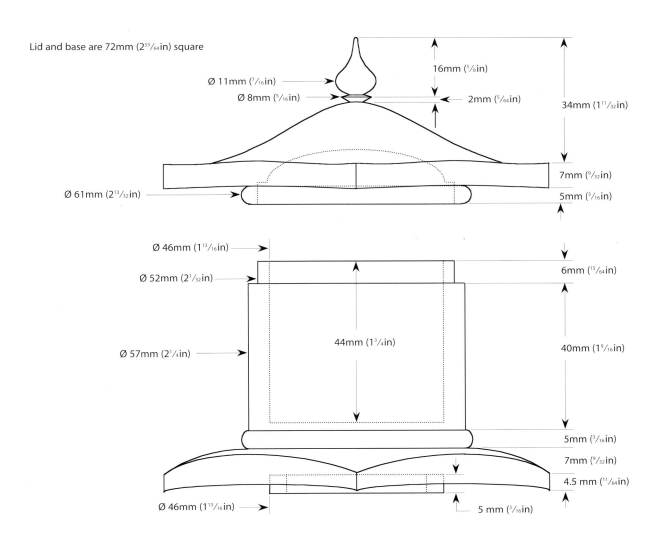

Lid and base are 72mm (2⁵³⁄₆₄in) square

Ø 11mm (⁷⁄₁₆in)

16mm (⁵⁄₈in)

Ø 8mm (⁵⁄₁₆in)

2mm (⁵⁄₆₄in)

34mm (1¹¹⁄₃₂in)

7mm (⁹⁄₃₂in)

Ø 61mm (2¹³⁄₃₂in)

5mm (³⁄₁₆in)

Ø 46mm (1¹³⁄₁₆in)

6mm (¹⁵⁄₆₄in)

Ø 52mm (2¹⁄₃₂in)

44mm (1³⁄₄in)

40mm (1⁹⁄₁₆in)

Ø 57mm (2¹⁄₄in)

5mm (³⁄₁₆in)

7mm (⁹⁄₃₂in)

4.5 mm (¹¹⁄₆₄in)

Ø 46mm (1¹³⁄₁₆in)

5 mm (³⁄₁₆in)

Box 26 | Pagoda box 103

Box 27

Bird-box ornament

Sycamore and purpleheart

h. 76mm (3in), max. d. 23mm ($^{29}/_{32}$in)

This little item is actually a Christmas-tree ornament, and its making is shown on my video *Inlaid & Novelty Boxes*. As it is really a box which has its lid glued on, I feel justified in including it here.

While the sycamore is still square, a hole should be drilled through one side to form the bird's entry point. Then, with the wood fitted into the chuck, a hole is drilled down the centre. The outside is then cut to give a fairly thin wall. All but the last point of the lower finial can be turned with a gouge, and the piece sanded, sealed and

polished. The last cut, to detach the base, is made with a skew, which gives a very clean cut ready for subsequent finishing by hand. The purpleheart top is turned in a similar manner, but before parting off, a small hole needs to be drilled through so that a loop fashioned from a paper clip can be glued in, allowing the ornament to be hung on a tree.

This is an item that can be turned quite quickly, and may well be a viable proposition for the Christmas market.

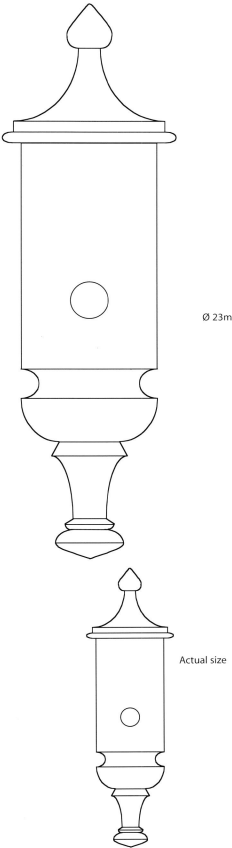

Bird-box ornament

Reproduced at twice actual size

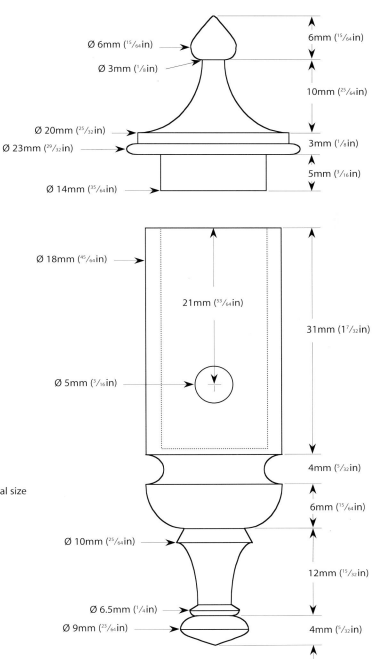

Ø 6mm ($^{15}/_{64}$in)

Ø 3mm ($^{1}/_{8}$in)

6mm ($^{15}/_{64}$in)

10mm ($^{25}/_{64}$in)

Ø 20mm ($^{25}/_{32}$in)

Ø 23mm ($^{29}/_{32}$in)

3mm ($^{1}/_{8}$in)

5mm ($^{3}/_{16}$in)

Ø 14mm ($^{35}/_{64}$in)

Ø 18mm ($^{45}/_{64}$in)

21mm ($^{53}/_{64}$in)

31mm ($1^{7}/_{32}$in)

Ø 5mm ($^{3}/_{16}$in)

4mm ($^{5}/_{32}$in)

6mm ($^{15}/_{64}$in)

Ø 10mm ($^{25}/_{64}$in)

12mm ($^{15}/_{32}$in)

Ø 6.5mm ($^{1}/_{4}$in)

Ø 9mm ($^{23}/_{64}$in)

4mm ($^{5}/_{32}$in)

Actual size

Box 27 | Bird-box ornament   105

Box 28

Bird box

Maple, sonokeling, lilac

h. 141mm (5⁹/₁₆ in), max. d. 65mm (2⁹/₁₆ in)

drilled through to take a wire loop, before reversing onto a jam chuck to complete the curve.

The base can then be turned to match, and to complete the piece small finials are made from an offcut of lilac. Once all the parts have been completed, the wire loop is fitted and the box is glued together.

If this project is scaled up to produce a full-sized nesting box, please omit the perch, as any bird taking up residence will not need it, but larger birds will use it as a foothold to rob the nest.

Variations

The version with a rounded profile has a more rustic and picturesque look to it. Another way of wiring this box is to drill across the finial and fit a wire loop, instead of drilling right down through the lid; this allows the finial to be brought to a point at the top.

This project is another Christmas-tree ornament, but is a little more involved than the previous one. It can be made much more attractive by using offcuts of different woods to create a nice contrast. In fact it is not a box at all, but because it needs similar techniques to make it, I have included it.

This piece is started by turning a tube for the body. The holes can be drilled while it is still square, or later on the pillar drill, supported by a vee-block.

The top, or roof, looks attractive with a downward-curving overhang, and this entails making sure that the spigot fits the tube, even when recessed. The solution is to cut a long spigot first, undercut the roof and then shorten the spigot. Remove as much of the inside of the roof as possible in order to reduce the weight. The roof needs to be

Round-bottomed variant in maple and padauk
h. 130mm (5¹/₈ in), max. d. 63mm (2³¹/₆₄ in)

Bird box

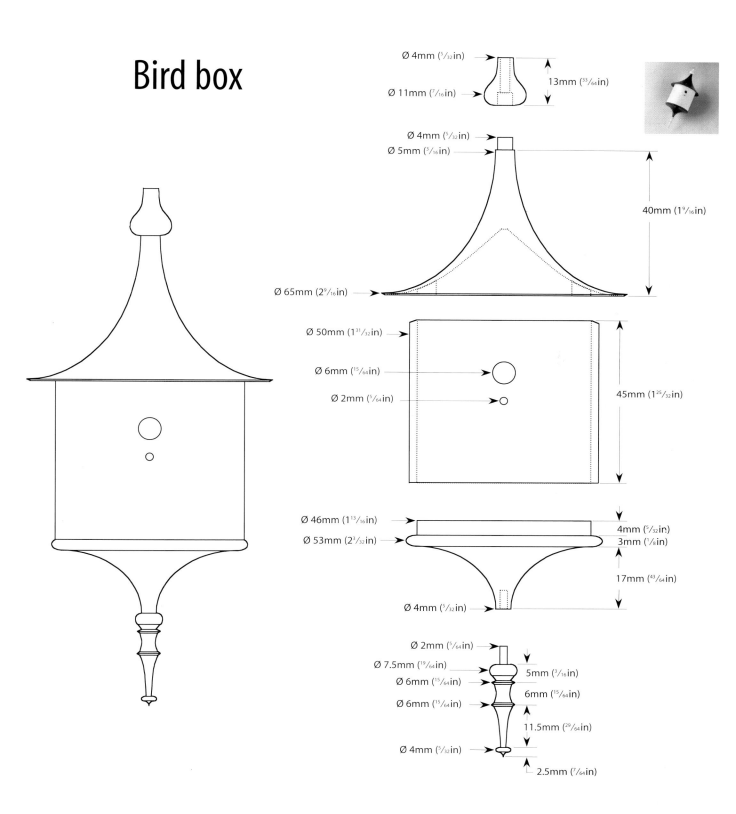

Ø 4mm (⁵/₃₂ in)

Ø 11mm (⁷/₁₆ in)

13mm (³³/₆₄ in)

Ø 4mm (⁵/₃₂ in)

Ø 5mm (³/₁₆ in)

40mm (1⁹/₁₆ in)

Ø 65mm (2⁹/₁₆ in)

Ø 50mm (1³¹/₃₂ in)

Ø 6mm (¹⁵/₆₄ in)

Ø 2mm (⁵/₆₄ in)

45mm (1²⁵/₃₂ in)

Ø 46mm (1¹³/₁₆ in)

Ø 53mm (2³/₃₂ in)

4mm (⁵/₃₂ in)

3mm (¹/₈ in)

17mm (⁴³/₆₄ in)

Ø 4mm (⁵/₃₂ in)

Ø 2mm (⁵/₆₄ in)

Ø 7.5mm (¹⁹/₆₄ in)

Ø 6mm (¹⁵/₆₄ in)

Ø 6mm (¹⁵/₆₄ in)

5mm (³/₁₆ in)

6mm (¹⁵/₆₄ in)

11.5mm (²⁹/₆₄ in)

Ø 4mm (⁵/₃₂ in)

2.5mm (⁷/₆₄ in)

Box 28 | Bird box   107

Box 29

Finial egg box
Rippled ash and ebony
h. 129mm (5³/₃₂ in), d. 49mm (1¹⁵/₁₆ in)

Black on white creates the strongest visual contrast possible, and it would be very easy for the ebony finial to overpower the white box, making it look top-heavy. Creating a balanced effect is critical in many of these projects.

Once again, the top part of the box was turned first, this time from rippled ash, a fairly coarse-grained wood, but one which turns easily and finishes well.

The main difficulty with this box is achieving a pleasing shape. The turner needs to visualize the whole curve whilst turning just the top part. Maybe the proportions of this box would have been improved if the join had been just a fraction higher. This would probably have given a more balanced effect.

If the lid is turned in stages – a little removed outside, then inside – it will reduce the chances of the scraper chattering as a thin wall is created. If the outer shape of the base is turned with the top in place, it is easier to create a better-shaped egg. Both parts need to be reverse-chucked to complete the top and base. The ebony finial can then be turned; it is important to create an accurate diameter and length on the spigot, as it will be glued into a very shallow recess on the box top.

Variation

In the variant shown at left, the finial extends inside the lid to give added interest to the interior.

Variation with finial extended inside, in ash and ebony
h. 140mm (5¹/₂ in), d. 56mm (2⁷/₃₂ in)

Finial egg box

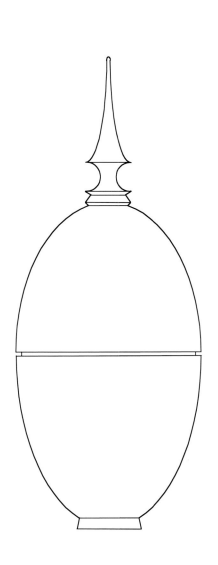

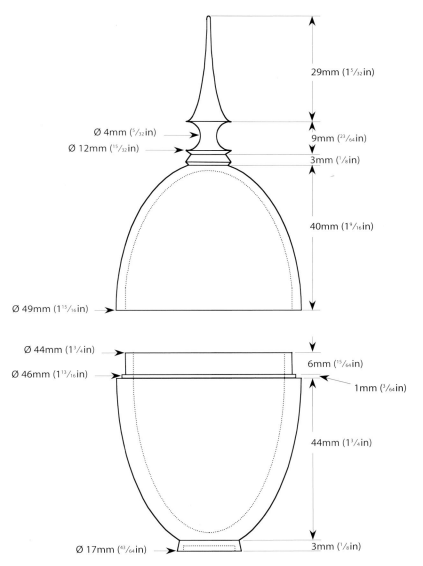

29mm (1⁵/₃₂in)

Ø 4mm (⁵/₃₂in)

Ø 12mm (¹⁵/₃₂in)

9mm (²³/₆₄in)

3mm (¹/₈in)

40mm (1⁹/₁₆in)

Ø 49mm (1¹⁵/₁₆in)

Ø 44mm (1³/₄in)

Ø 46mm (1¹³/₁₆in)

6mm (¹⁵/₆₄in)

1mm (³/₆₄in)

44mm (1³/₄in)

Ø 17mm (⁴³/₆₄in)

3mm (¹/₈in)

Box 29 | Finial egg box   109

Box 30

Tipsy boxes 1 and 2

1: Sycamore

h. 61.5mm ($2^{27}/_{64}$ in), d. 67mm ($2^5/_8$ in)

2: Ash

h. 50mm ($1^{31}/_{32}$ in), d. 71mm ($2^{51}/_{64}$ in)

On the first box I put the spigot on the base and this created some problems; so on the second box the spigot is on the lid.

This is a style of box that I really enjoy making. The inspiration came from a picture in a German magazine that I was given some years ago. It requires the use of the Ron French Variant eccentric chuck, or something comparable, to create the offset base.

The inside of the top can be turned in the normal manner, taking care to make it as near a hemisphere as possible. It is then reverse-chucked on a scrap block to complete the shape and polish it. The spigot, and the recess in the base, are then turned and polished. With a waste block mounted on the Variant chuck, a spigot is turned to fit the recess. Now comes the tricky bit: a recess has to be turned in the waste block to accommodate the spigot on the base, to allow the face of the base to fit flush against the block. This gives the support needed to turn the base curve. The waste block is now moved over on the eccentric chuck, by half the diameter of the lid. Although the block and the box base will now rotate eccentrically, the centre can still be supported by the tailstock, allowing the turning of the hemispherical base without much trouble.

Following the little problem with the spigot on the base, I rethought the process and turned another box. This time I put the spigot on the lid. Now a spigot can be turned on the waste block, and the top face of the base will rest against the surface of the block. This box is made in ash and coloured black and yellow with acrylic paint.

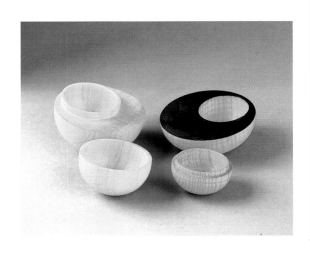

Tipsy boxes 1 and 2

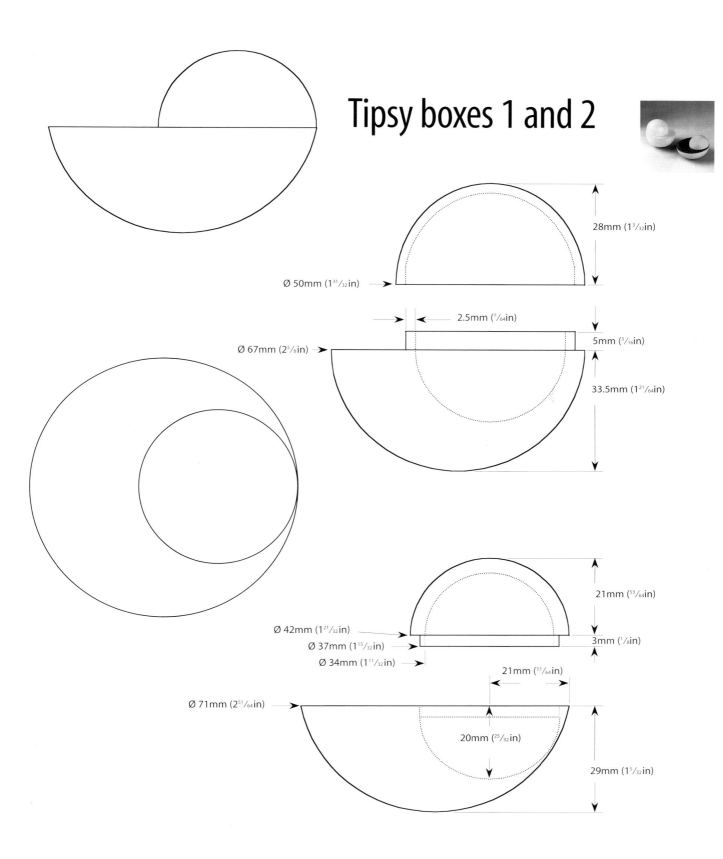

28mm (1³/₃₂in)

Ø 50mm (1³¹/₃₂in)

2.5mm (⁷/₆₄in)

Ø 67mm (2⁵/₈in)

5mm (³/₁₆in)

33.5mm (1²¹/₆₄in)

21mm (⁵³/₆₄in)

Ø 42mm (1²¹/₃₂in)

Ø 37mm (1¹⁵/₃₂in)

3mm (¹/₈in)

Ø 34mm (1¹¹/₃₂in)

21mm (⁵³/₆₄in)

Ø 71mm (2⁵¹/₆₄in)

20mm (²⁵/₃₂in)

29mm (1⁵/₃₂in)

Box 30 | Tipsy boxes 1 and 2   111

Box 31

Trinket box

Burr elm, sycamore, ebony

h. 148.5mm (5^{27}/$_{32}$in), d. 98mm (3^{55}/$_{64}$in)

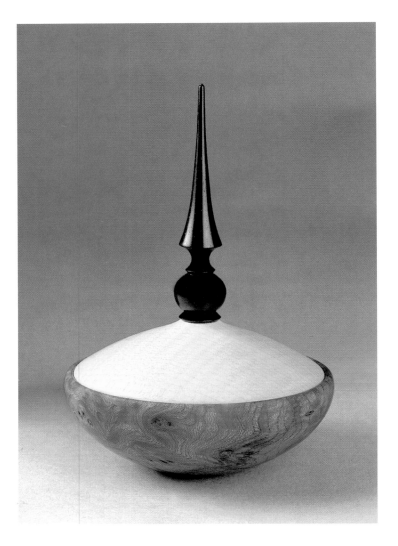

I had accumulated a large number of small, rough-turned burr-elm bowls, that had been kiln-dried many years ago. These had not been turned to a finish, because they were only about 100mm (4in) in diameter, and as such were not really profitable. However, I felt that if they could somehow be converted into boxes, they might become a more attractive proposition.

The first step is to mount the rough bowl between a waste block and the tailstock, in order to recut the bottom spigot. With this held in the chuck, the outside can be shaped as far as it is possible to reach, using a 6mm (¼in) bowl gouge. The rim of the bowl is rounded, and there is a small ridge inside for the lid to sit on. This can be cut using a small spindle gouge and a square scraper. The remainder of the interior is removed with the same 6mm bowl gouge, then sanded and finally polished.

To complete the outside, the inner ridge is gripped on the expanding jaws of the four-jaw chuck. This allows the turning of the outer curve and foot unhindered by the tailstock. With the base finished, attention can be focused on the lid.

A block of sycamore (or other contrasting wood) is mounted in the lathe and the diameter turned to fit the recess in the base. A domed shape complements the base nicely, but such a shape is hard to grip on the inside when turning the top. A tiny bead (shown inset in the working drawing), about a third of the way up the curve, solves the problem, as the chuck jaws can expand onto the inside of this bead. This allows the turning of the top curve, and the small recess for the knob.

I have made boxes using the same basic design with a round knob on top, but in this instance I wanted something a little more impressive, so I turned the ebony spire which was then glued into the small recess in the lid. Some customers tell me they use the spire as a ring holder.

Trinket box

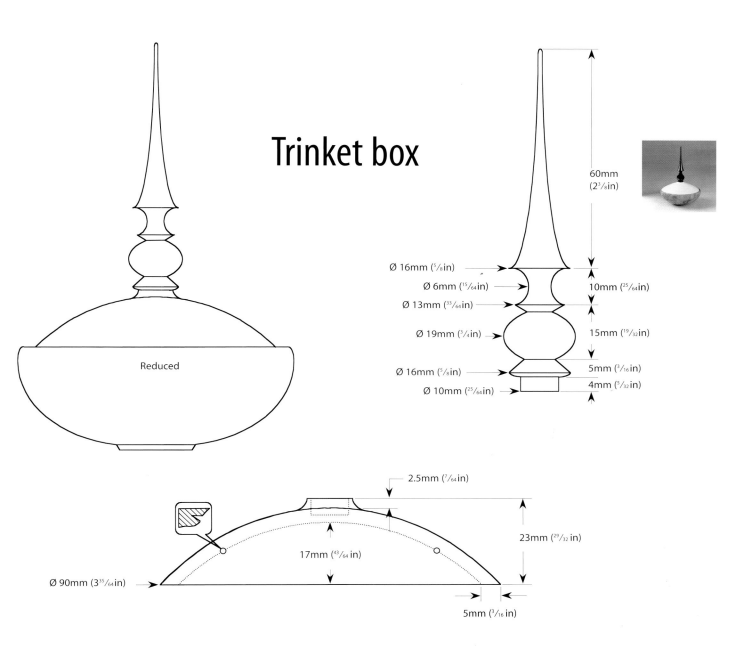

Reduced

60mm (2³/₈in)

Ø 16mm (⁵/₈in)
Ø 6mm (¹⁵/₆₄in)
Ø 13mm (³³/₆₄in)
Ø 19mm (³/₄in)
Ø 16mm (⁵/₈in)
Ø 10mm (²⁵/₆₄in)

10mm (²⁵/₆₄in)
15mm (¹⁹/₃₂in)
5mm (³/₁₆in)
4mm (⁵/₃₂in)

2.5mm (⁷/₆₄in)
23mm (²⁹/₃₂in)
17mm (⁴³/₆₄in)
Ø 90mm (3³⁵/₆₄in)
5mm (³/₁₆in)

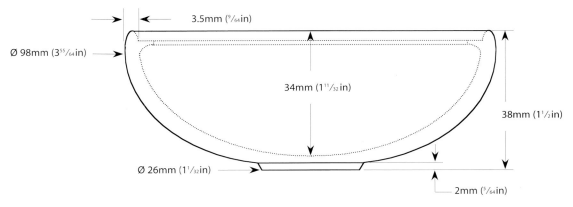

3.5mm (⁹/₆₄in)
Ø 98mm (3⁵⁵/₆₄in)
34mm (1¹¹/₃₂in)
38mm (1¹/₂in)
Ø 26mm (1¹/₃₂in)
2mm (⁵/₆₄in)

Box 31 | Trinket box   113

Box 32

Seattle Tower box

Rippled ash, pink ivory, amarello, ebony

h. 206mm (8$\frac{1}{8}$ in), d. 72mm (2$\frac{53}{64}$ in)

This box, not surprisingly, was inspired by seeing the Space Needle on a visit to Seattle, USA. I felt that the elegant shape could be converted to a box, with just a little artistic licence.

The starting point is the central box portion in pink ivory. This is held in the chuck, the outside shape turned and the inside removed using my miniature hollow-form tools (see page 17). By reverse-chucking onto a scrap block, the spigot can then be removed and a recess created to mate with the tower.

Working the amarello lid comes next. The underside and the outside diameter are turned to match the box's opening, and to complete the top surface it can be jam-chucked into a recess in a waste block.

The tall spire in ebony needs to be very slender, otherwise it will overpower the whole effect. This requires some very delicate work with the 13mm ($\frac{1}{2}$in) skew. It is amazing just how strong ebony is, even at 2mm ($\frac{5}{64}$ in) thickness.

Finally the ash tower is made, by first cutting a spigot to fit into the base of the pink ivory box and then cutting the long curve down to the base of the tower. The tower can be drilled down the centre, thereby making the project into a double box. Finally the tower is reverse-chucked to remove the holding spigot and finish the base.

Seattle Tower box

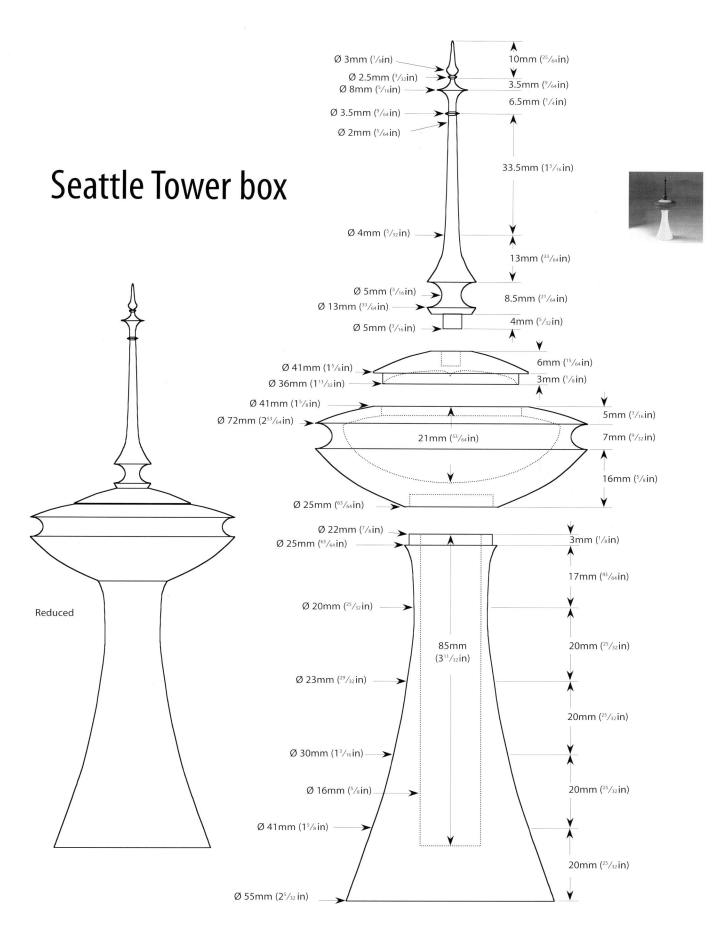

Ø 3mm (¹⁄₈in)
10mm (²⁵⁄₆₄in)
Ø 2.5mm (³⁄₃₂in)
3.5mm (⁹⁄₆₄in)
Ø 8mm (⁵⁄₁₆in)
6.5mm (¹⁄₄in)
Ø 3.5mm (⁹⁄₆₄in)
Ø 2mm (⁵⁄₆₄in)

33.5mm (1⁵⁄₁₆in)

Ø 4mm (⁵⁄₃₂in)

13mm (³³⁄₆₄in)

Ø 5mm (³⁄₁₆in)
8.5mm (²¹⁄₆₄in)
Ø 13mm (³³⁄₆₄in)
Ø 5mm (³⁄₁₆in)
4mm (⁵⁄₃₂in)

Ø 41mm (1⁵⁄₈in)
6mm (¹⁵⁄₆₄in)
Ø 36mm (1¹³⁄₃₂in)
3mm (¹⁄₈in)

Ø 41mm (1⁵⁄₈in)
5mm (³⁄₁₆in)
Ø 72mm (2⁵³⁄₆₄in)
21mm (⁵³⁄₆₄in)
7mm (⁹⁄₃₂in)

16mm (⁵⁄₈in)

Ø 25mm (⁶³⁄₆₄in)

Reduced

Ø 22mm (⁷⁄₈in)
Ø 25mm (⁶³⁄₆₄in)
3mm (¹⁄₈in)

17mm (⁴³⁄₆₄in)

Ø 20mm (²⁵⁄₃₂in)

20mm (²⁵⁄₃₂in)

85mm
(3¹¹⁄₃₂in)

Ø 23mm (²⁹⁄₃₂in)

20mm (²⁵⁄₃₂in)

Ø 30mm (1³⁄₁₆in)

20mm (²⁵⁄₃₂in)

Ø 16mm (⁵⁄₈in)

Ø 41mm (1⁵⁄₈in)

20mm (²⁵⁄₃₂in)

Ø 55mm (2⁵⁄₃₂in)

Box 32 | Seattle Tower box   115

Box 33

UFO box

Bird's-eye maple and Santos rosewood

h. 73mm (2⁷⁄₈in), d. 130mm (5¹⁄₈in)

This box was made with only one object in mind: to show off the bird's-eye maple in the best possible way. The timber only shows its figure when the wood is cut parallel to the grain, so this box had to be turned side grain, as opposed to end grain, as in most of the other projects. This can create problems, especially when hollowing. In this box, I have used a very simple format to overcome these difficulties. Fortunately bird's-eye maple is more likely to be available in the small bowl blank form used here than in squares.

The face showing the best figure is selected, and drilled for a screw chuck. Mounted in this way, underside and spigot are turned. Whilst held on this spigot, the top face is turned, as well as the spigot for locating the lid, and the simple recess.

(Note: this is also a good, quick way of turning small bowls where the face of the timber shows interesting grain.)

The base is then reverse-chucked onto a waste block for the chuck spigot to be removed and the bottom completed.

The top is turned on end grain, making sure that the inside is hemispherical, and most of the outside shape can be cut as well before parting off. It is then jam-chucked and completed. Due to the shape of the lid, the fit needs to be easy rather than tight.

Variations

There are many variations possible with this design: thinner timber could be used for the base, and the lid could be modified into almost any shape.

UFO box

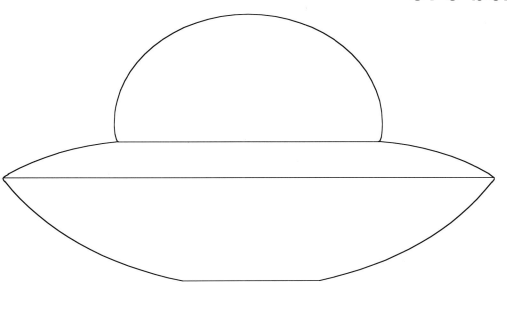

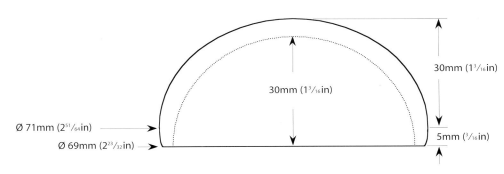

Ø 71mm (2⁵¹/₆₄in)

Ø 69mm (2²³/₃₂in)

30mm (1³/₁₆in)

30mm (1³/₁₆in)

5mm (³/₁₆in)

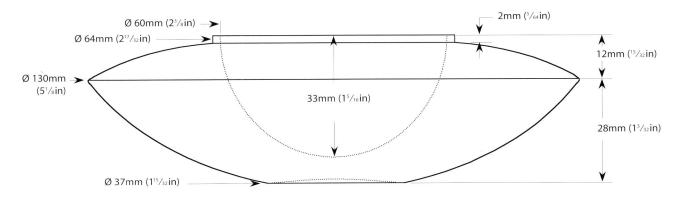

Ø 60mm (2³/₈in)

Ø 64mm (2¹⁷/₃₂in)

Ø 130mm (5¹/₈in)

Ø 37mm (1¹⁵/₃₂in)

2mm (⁵/₆₄in)

12mm (¹⁵/₃₂in)

33mm (1⁵/₁₆in)

28mm (1³/₃₂in)

Box 33 | UFO box   117

Box 34

Galaxy box

Box elder burl and ebony

h. 101mm (3⁶³⁄₆₄ in), d. 120mm (4²³⁄₃₂ in)

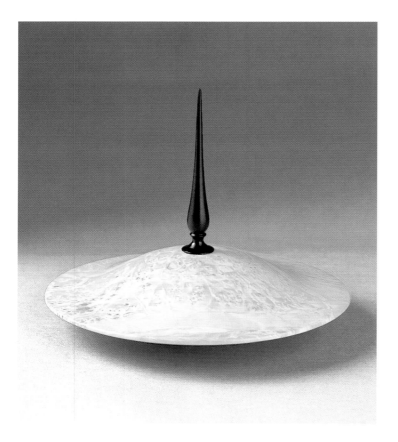

This box was inspired by a photograph taken with the Hubble telescope. It is of the distant galaxy M87, said to have a giant black hole at its core which causes a jet of matter to be expelled from the centre to travel millions of miles into space. Artistic licence allows the box elder burl, with its many 'eyes', to represent the body of the galaxy, and a spire of ebony to represent the jet ejected by the black hole.

The body of the box is made from a 127 x 51mm (5 x 2in) bowl blank. The best side is selected for the lid and top. A block can be glued onto this face and drilled for a screw chuck. Now the basic shape can be turned and a spigot created on the base, making sure enough material has been left for the lid. With the piece held on this spigot, the shape is refined and the lid portion parted off. Hollowing is relatively simple, as the wood is quite soft and cuts cleanly with sharp tools. The undercut scraper allows shaping of the inside without the need to penetrate too far into the 'wings'. The recess needs a tiny shelf to support the lid, and this is now cut.

The inner surface of the lid is cut, the hole drilled for the spire, and the diameter is reduced until it is a tight fit in the base. With the base remounted in the chuck and the lid in place, the upper curve can be cut. This can only be done if the lid is a tight fit; however, after finishing it is then virtually impossible to remove the lid without damaging it.

With a piece of ebony in the chuck, a small spigot can be turned to fit the hole in the lid. After gluing it into the hole, it is possible to pull off the lid. Cleaning up the underside of the lid comes next, and then turning as much of the spire as possible. The final cuts to the end of the spire are taken with the lid jam-chucked into a recess on a waste block. Finally the base is jam-chucked on a waste block to remove the spigot and shape the underside.

As with all previous boxes, the sanding, sealing and polishing have to be done as you go along; otherwise you may finish up with one part of the box unfinished and no means of holding it.

There may well be other ways of approaching this project – if you can see one, go ahead and do whatever works for you. Quite often a problem will dictate the way you go, as with the jammed lid. There is never one right way, only a series of possibilities.

Galaxy box

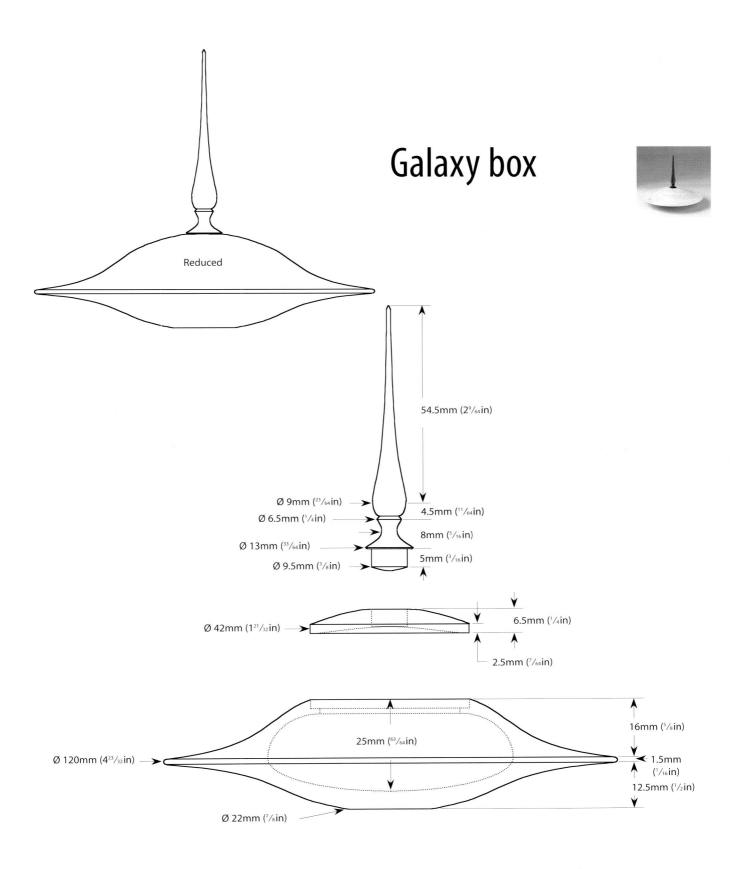

Reduced

54.5mm ($2^9/_{64}$in)

Ø 9mm ($^{23}/_{64}$in)

Ø 6.5mm ($^1/_4$in)

4.5mm ($^{11}/_{64}$in)

8mm ($^5/_{16}$in)

Ø 13mm ($^{33}/_{64}$in)

Ø 9.5mm ($^3/_8$in)

5mm ($^3/_{16}$in)

Ø 42mm ($1^{21}/_{32}$in)

6.5mm ($^1/_4$in)

2.5mm ($^7/_{64}$in)

16mm ($^5/_8$in)

25mm ($^{63}/_{64}$in)

Ø 120mm ($4^{23}/_{32}$in)

1.5mm ($^1/_{16}$in)

12.5mm ($^1/_2$in)

Ø 22mm ($^7/_8$in)

Box 34 | Galaxy box   119

Box 35

Clam box

Camphor

h. 26mm (1 $\frac{1}{32}$ in), d. 73mm (2 $\frac{7}{8}$ in)

Ray Key makes a clam box with a much more pronounced curve to the top and bottom, and this makes the recess at the edge much tighter.
In order to avoid a direct copy, I have made this box with a larger inward curve at the edge, and a shallower curve to top and base.

Once the basic steps in box making have been mastered, this is a very straightforward design, and should present very few problems.

As long as the top and base curves are kept similar, and the deep curve at the opening follows through the join, this box looks well in a wood that has interesting end grain.

The only problems I encountered during making were due to the soft nature of the camphor wood that I used. This has a very open grain and, as most of the box shows end grain, I had to apply several coats of sealer to achieve a good finish.

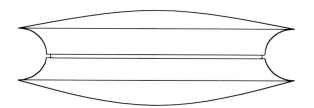

Clam box

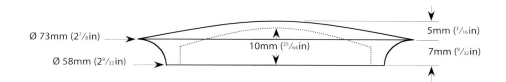

Ø 73mm (2⁷⁄₈in)

Ø 58mm (2⁹⁄₃₂in)

10mm (²⁵⁄₆₄in)

5mm (³⁄₁₆in)

7mm (⁹⁄₃₂in)

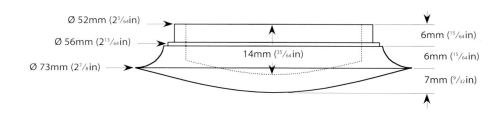

Ø 52mm (2³⁄₆₄in)

Ø 56mm (2¹³⁄₆₄in)

Ø 73mm (2⁷⁄₈in)

14mm (³⁵⁄₆₄in)

6mm (¹⁵⁄₆₄in)

6mm (¹⁵⁄₆₄in)

7mm (⁹⁄₃₂in)

Detail on base

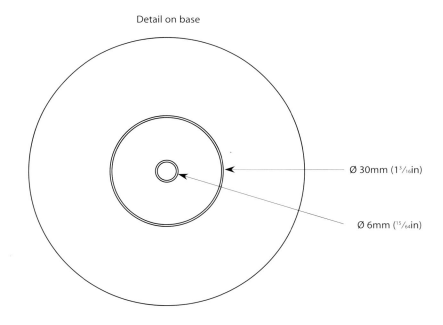

Ø 30mm (1³⁄₁₆in)

Ø 6mm (¹⁵⁄₆₄in)

Box 35 | Clam box 121

Box 36

Skep or beehive box

Olive

h. 60mm (2³/₈ in), d. 59mm (2¹¹/₃₂ in)

I have never seen a traditional skep, other than as a drawing in a book. However, as I understand it, they are constructed from a 'rope' of straw. This is what I have tried to show by making the diameter of the 'rope' diminish towards the top of the hive.

Due to the tapered shape of the profile I had to construct the box with the locating spigot on the lid, rather than on the base. If I had used my normal format, with the spigot on the base, it would have made the lid much thicker than the base.

This box can be started by turning the lower part. As the bottom is the widest part of the box there is plenty of support when hollowing. The only difficulty is dividing the outer profile into the diminishing beads and making sure that the opening is situated between two of these. Another point to watch is that the sides of the base opening must be parallel, so as to locate with the spigot for the lid.

When the lower part has been reverse-chucked and completely finished, the lid portion can be held in the chuck, and the spigot cut to fit the base. As the profile of the lid reduces in diameter towards the top, it is advisable to hollow it in stages. Also, make sure that the initial opening is parallel so that it can be jam-chucked onto a spigot to complete the top bead; otherwise it will have to be jam-chucked into a recess, which is slightly more difficult.

This was quite a satisfying box to make; the fact that the opening is disguised by the beads makes it more visually interesting.

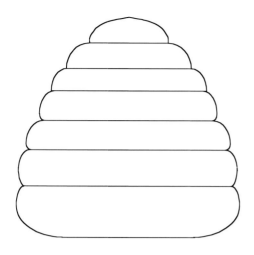

Skep or beehive box

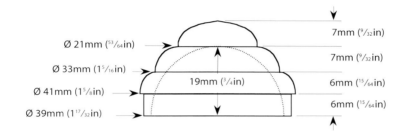

Ø 21mm (⁵³/₆₄in) →   7mm (⁹/₃₂in)

Ø 33mm (1⁵/₁₆in) →   7mm (⁹/₃₂in)

                     19mm (³/₄in)   6mm (¹⁵/₆₄in)

Ø 41mm (1⁵/₈in) →

Ø 39mm (1¹⁷/₃₂in) →   6mm (¹⁵/₆₄in)

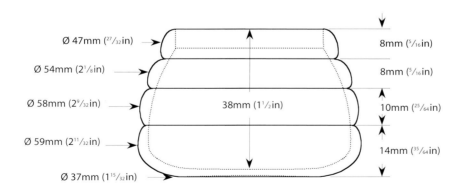

Ø 47mm (²⁷/₃₂in) →   8mm (⁵/₁₆in)

Ø 54mm (2¹/₈in) →   8mm (⁵/₁₆in)

Ø 58mm (2⁹/₃₂in) →   38mm (1¹/₂in)   10mm (²⁵/₆₄in)

Ø 59mm (2¹¹/₃₂in) →

                                         14mm (³⁵/₆₄in)

Ø 37mm (1¹⁵/₃₂in) →

Box 36 | Skep or beehive box   123

Box 37

Inset-lid box

Ebony and chittam burl

h. 72mm (2$^{27}/_{32}$ in), d. 53mm (2$^{3}/_{32}$ in)

This is another box that uses the contrast of colours to create an impact. It also uses the basic egg shape that I like so much, but this time it is slightly elongated.

Turning starts with forming the outside shape of the box part, leaving a little extra 'meat' at the base until hollowing has been completed. The top edge of the base needs to be rounded, to form a bead intended to frame the inset lid. Create a step for the lid to sit on and then undercut below this to avoid leaving the walls too thick. A little extra thickness in the base is all right, as this increases stability.

This design needs a thin lid, so the knob spigot is taken right through, and this actually helps during the turning. When turning the underside of the lid, reduce the diameter to fit the base, drill the hole and polish, before parting off the disc. A recess can be cut in a piece of scrap to hold the lid, and the top surface completed.

With a length of ebony in the chuck, a spigot can be cut to fit the hole in the lid, and the knob shaped. The lid is now glued onto this spigot and the protruding end on the underside is trimmed and polished. After parting off the knob, the lid can be jam-chucked on the waste block again in order to complete the top of the knob.

Variations

The design can be varied to suit the wood in hand. It can be made taller or shorter, and the contrasting woods mixed and matched.

Far left: Ebony and amarello; h. 76mm (3in), d. 50mm (13$^{1}/_{32}$in) Near left: Ebony and cocobolo; h. 76mm (3in), d. 56mm (2$^{3}/_{16}$ in)

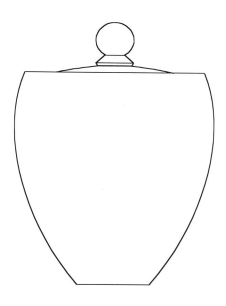

Inset-lid box

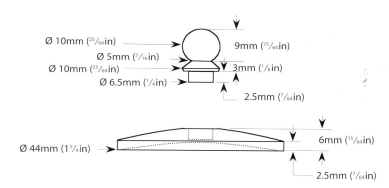

Ø 10mm (²⁵/₆₄in)
Ø 5mm (³/₁₆in)
Ø 10mm (²⁵/₆₄in)
Ø 6.5mm (¹/₄in)

9mm (²³/₆₄in)
3mm (¹/₈in)
2.5mm (⁷/₆₄in)

Ø 44mm (1³/₄in)

6mm (¹⁵/₆₄in)
2.5mm (⁷/₆₄in)

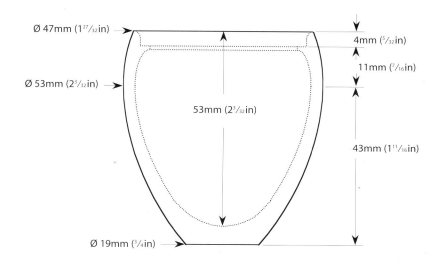

Ø 47mm (1²⁷/₃₂in)
Ø 53mm (2³/₃₂in)
53mm (2³/₃₂in)
Ø 19mm (³/₄in)

4mm (⁵/₃₂in)
11mm (⁷/₁₆in)
43mm (1¹¹/₁₆in)

Box 37 | Inset-lid box   125

Box 38

Double-decker box
Maple and bubinga

h. 78.5mm (3³/₃₂ in), d. 71mm (2⁵¹/₆₄ in)

This is another box that I made for my video *Inlaid & Novelty Boxes*. One unusual feature is that there are rings of a contrasting wood inlaid into the side as well as the lid of this box. The details of this procedure were given on page 38.

This box is made in what must now be a familiar manner, with the inside of the lid completed first. This is then jam-chucked on the box spigot to finish the outside.

Hollowing the top box requires a little more care, as it is worked a long way out from the chuck. This increases the leverage, and there is a risk of pulling the wood out of the chuck. With the inside completed, the depth is measured

and an allowance made for the recess underneath. The top box is then parted off and jam-chucked onto a waste block for the underside to be turned. This will become the lid for the lower box.

With this finished, the lower box spigot is turned to fit the upper box, and the lower box hollowed. Careful measuring is required to make sure that the two boxes are the same height when fitted together. Finally the bottom box is jam-chucked to complete the underside.

After making this box I started thinking that there must be an easier way. The following Four-Stack box was the result of this thought process.

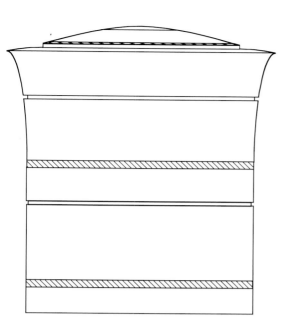

Double-decker box

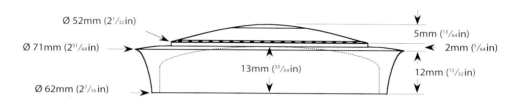

Ø 52mm (2¹/₃₂in)
Ø 71mm (2⁵¹/₆₄in)
Ø 62mm (2⁷/₁₆in)
13mm (³³/₆₄in)
5mm (¹³/₆₄in)
2mm (⁵/₆₄in)
12mm (¹⁵/₃₂in)

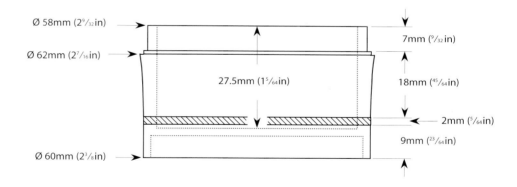

Ø 58mm (2⁹/₃₂in)
Ø 62mm (2⁷/₁₆in)
27.5mm (1⁵/₆₄in)
Ø 60mm (2³/₈in)
7mm (⁹/₃₂in)
18mm (⁴⁵/₆₄in)
2mm (⁵/₆₄in)
9mm (²³/₆₄in)

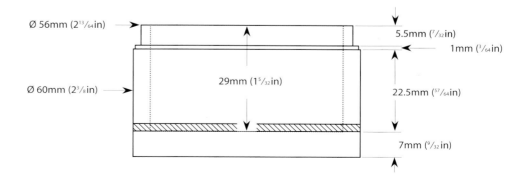

Ø 56mm (2¹³/₆₄in)
Ø 60mm (2³/₈in)
29mm (1⁵/₃₂in)
5.5mm (⁷/₃₂in)
1mm (³/₆₄in)
22.5mm (⁵⁷/₆₄in)
7mm (⁹/₃₂in)

Box 38 | Double-decker box   127

Box 39

Four-stack box

Rippled ash

h. 115mm (4¹⁷/₃₂ in), d. 65mm (2⁹/₁₆ in)

The techniques used in the making of this set of boxes grew out of the problems that students have experienced when making the Double-Decker box. Although I have made this box only four compartments high, the same methods could be used for any reasonable number of boxes. Alternatively the outer profile, which in this case is like the old-fashioned pillar box (public mailbox), could, with a little thought and planning, be made almost any shape.

With a length of roughed-round timber fitted in the chuck, mark off the height of the bottom box, that is, the one nearest to the chuck. At this point another chucking spigot about 6mm wide (just under ¼ in) needs to be cut. From the top of this spigot the second box is measured, and another chucking spigot cut. This is repeated up the timber until four boxes and a lid have been marked out, all with their respective spigots. It is a good idea to

number them in pencil at this point, to avoid mistakes later on. I made the bottom box no. 1.

Now each element is parted off, making sure that each box has its spigot on the lower end, and the final lid has a spigot on top. With the bottom box still in the chuck, this is now hollowed, sanded and polished inside. Each box in turn can now be held securely in the chuck for hollowing. If vernier callipers are used to make all the recesses the same it will simplify things later.

When all the boxes have been hollowed, the lid portion is fitted into the chuck and turned to fit the top box (no. 4 in my case). With box 4 in the chuck, the lid can be fitted and the top surface completed. At this point the outside of box 4 can be cut to its final diameter.

With a waste block in the chuck, a spigot is cut to fit inside box 2. The chucking spigot can then be reduced to fit into the top of box 1, and the inside of this spigot recessed, sanded and polished. Then box 3 is treated in a similar manner, and made to fit the top of box 2. Box 4 follows the same path.

With box 4 still on the spigot, all the boxes are assembled in order. The bottom box (1) is the only one to retain a chucking point and, as it also still has a centre mark underneath, the tailstock can be brought up to support the assembled stack. Now the final diameter of the stack can be turned to match box 4, and all the outsides sanded and polished.

Finally, box 1 is jam-chucked to remove the chucking point, and the underside sanded and polished.

The above sounds very involved on first reading; however, it is all fairly straightforward when taken one step at a time.

Four-stack box

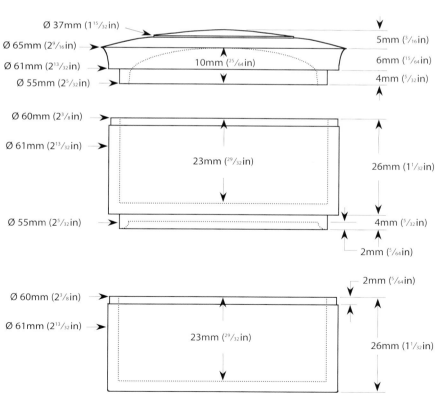

Ø 37mm ($1^{15}/_{32}$ in)

Ø 65mm ($2^9/_{16}$ in)

Ø 61mm ($2^{13}/_{32}$ in)

Ø 55mm ($2^5/_{32}$ in)

5mm ($^3/_{16}$ in)

10mm ($^{25}/_{64}$ in)

6mm ($^{15}/_{64}$ in)

4mm ($^5/_{32}$ in)

Ø 60mm ($2^3/_8$ in)

Ø 61mm ($2^{13}/_{32}$ in)

Ø 55mm ($2^5/_{32}$ in)

23mm ($^{29}/_{32}$ in)

26mm ($1^1/_{32}$ in)

4mm ($^5/_{32}$ in)

2mm ($^5/_{64}$ in)

Ø 60mm ($2^3/_8$ in)

Ø 61mm ($2^{13}/_{32}$ in)

2mm ($^5/_{64}$ in)

23mm ($^{29}/_{32}$ in)

26mm ($1^1/_{32}$ in)

Box 39 | Four-stack box 129

Box 40

Commissionaire box
Syringa
h. 45.5mm (1$^{25}/_{32}$ in), d. 68mm (2$^{11}/_{16}$ in)

When Alan Neal drew the plan for this box he noted that the profile looked like a commissionaire's hat. It is, in effect, a Clam box (see no. 35) with the top and bottom surfaces offset. This requires the use of a chuck where the centre can be moved, such as the Sorby or Variant eccentric chucks shown on page 13.

The initial turning of the inside is exactly the same as for the Clam box, except for the curve on the edge. In this design the top and bottom need to be thicker to allow for the offset cuts on the outside. I left approximately 3mm ($^1/_8$ in) more depth; if this is not done there is a strong possibility of cutting through on the edge and leaving a hole in the box.

With a piece of soft waste wood mounted on the screw of the offset chuck, a spigot can be turned to fit the lid of the box. Reference points are marked, on opposite sides of the block but parallel to the axis on which the screw moves, and numbered 1 and 2. This is so that the grain can be matched even though the top and base are offset in opposite directions.

With the top mounted on the spigot, and a feature in the grain aligned with point 1, the centre needs to be moved over by half the amount of the desired offset, and a reference mark made on the chuck. This ensures that the amount of offset can be repeated on the base of the box. It is also necessary to tape the lid to the block with masking tape to stop it creeping round as the top surface is turned.

With the initial cuts on the top the gouge will be cutting more air than wood. Although the traditional instructions for spindle turning tell us to rub the bevel at all times, with offset turning you have to just skim the surface with the bevel; otherwise the tool is bounced by the intermittent contact with the wood. Apart from this, turning the curve is fairly simple. Any ridges left by the bouncing of the tool can be easily removed by sanding with the lathe switched off. The little piece of wood left at the centre as the top curve is completed can be turned into a small finial; this will accentuate the off-centre effect.

To make the base, the block on the chuck needs to be returned to the true centre and a spigot cut to match the inside of the base. With the chosen grain feature aligned with point 2, the base is taped onto the spigot and the centre moved over by the same amount as before. Turning the base is just the same as for the lid. A tiny flat can be cut in the middle so that the box will sit without rocking, but this is optional. Obviously, the more the centre is moved, the more pronounced the off-centre effect will be.

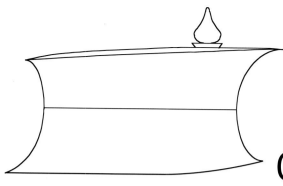

Commissionaire box

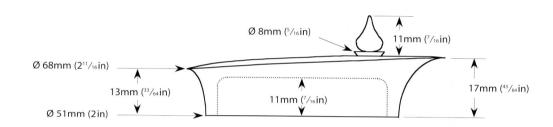

Ø 8mm (⁵/₁₆in)

11mm (⁷/₁₆in)

Ø 68mm (2¹¹/₁₆in)

13mm (³³/₆₄in)

Ø 51mm (2in)

11mm (⁷/₁₆in)

17mm (⁴³/₆₄in)

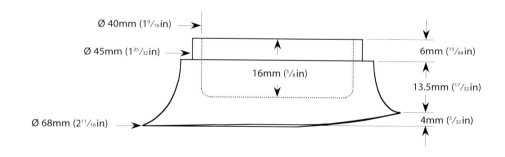

Ø 40mm (1⁹/₁₆in)

Ø 45mm (1²⁵/₃₂in)

16mm (⁵/₈in)

6mm (¹⁵/₆₄in)

13.5mm (¹⁷/₃₂in)

Ø 68mm (2¹¹/₁₆in)

4mm (⁵/₃₂in)

Variations

An interesting effect can be achieved by having both wings pointing in the same direction, and a more effective 'commissionaire's hat' created by modifying the shape of the base.

A more hat-like variant in imbuya
h. 33mm (1⁵/₁₆ in), d. 73mm (2⁷/₈ in)

Box 41

Top hat box

Ebony

h. 36.5mm (1$^{7}/_{16}$ in), d. 57mm (2$^{1}/_{4}$ in)

This box and the next two are made in the same way. The crowns are the lids and the brims are the bases.

The lid is turned first, the basic outer shape and the hollowing being done alternately in stages so that a thin wall can be created. As the brim has such a small spigot it will offer little to grip on, so it is better to reverse-chuck the crown onto a scrap spigot to complete the top curves.

The top surface of the brim can be turned next. Being end grain and quite thin, it is fragile. Before attempting to turn the underside, the brim should be jam-chucked into a waste block that supports the outer profile of the brim.

Top hat box

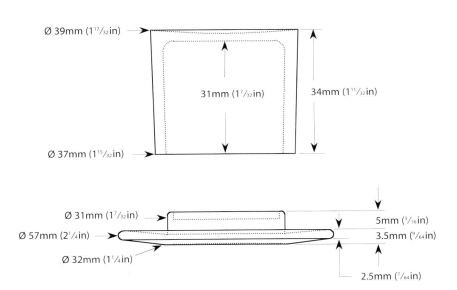

Ø 39mm (1¹⁷/₃₂in)

31mm (1⁷/₃₂in)

34mm (1¹¹/₃₂in)

Ø 37mm (1¹⁵/₃₂in)

Ø 31mm (1⁷/₃₂in)

Ø 57mm (2¹/₄in)

Ø 32mm (1¹/₄in)

5mm (³/₁₆in)

3.5mm (⁹/₆₄in)

2.5mm (⁷/₆₄in)

Box 41 | Top hat box   133

Box 42

Bowler hat box

Ebony

h. 27.5mm (1³⁄₃₂ in), d. 56mm (2¹³⁄₆₄ in)

This bowler hat (derby) is made in exactly the same way as the Top Hat box.

Variation

A ladies' straw boater, trimmed with a narrow ribbon, could also be made by the same method.

Actual size

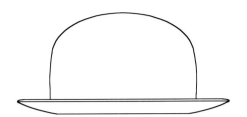

Bowler hat box

Reproduced at twice actual size

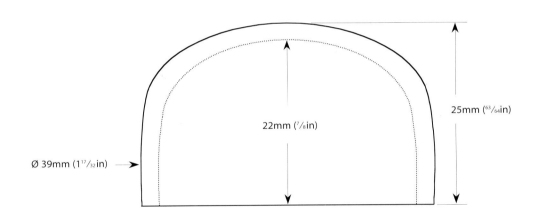

25mm ($^{63}/_{64}$in)

22mm ($^7/_8$in)

Ø 39mm (1$^{17}/_{32}$in) →

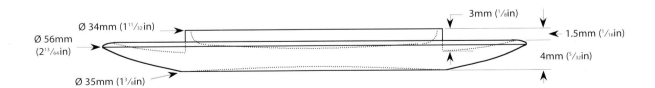

Ø 34mm (1$^{11}/_{32}$in)

Ø 56mm
(2$^{13}/_{64}$in)

Ø 35mm (1$^3/_8$in)

3mm ($^1/_8$in)

1.5mm ($^1/_{16}$in)

4mm ($^5/_{32}$in)

Box 42 | Bowler hat box

135

Box 43

Jockey cap box
Bubinga
h. 28mm (1⁷⁄₆₄ in), l. 63.5mm (2¹⁄₂ in)

The hat is first made with a circular brim, using the same method as for the Top Hat. The peak is then marked out on the brim, and the area shaded on the drawing is carefully cut away on the bandsaw. The edges are trimmed on the belt sander before hand-finishing.

Variations

Baseball caps in your local team colours would also be possible, but might require the use of dyes.

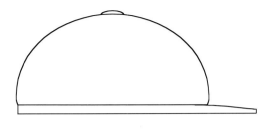

Jockey cap box

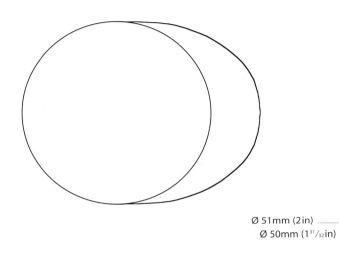

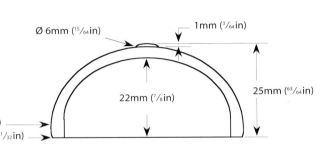

Ø 6mm ($^{15}/_{64}$in) 1mm ($^3/_{64}$in)

25mm ($^{63}/_{64}$in)

22mm ($^7/_8$in)

Ø 51mm (2in)
Ø 50mm (1$^{31}/_{32}$in)

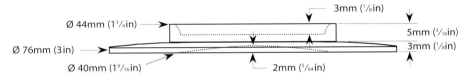

3mm ($^1/_8$in)

Ø 44mm (1$^3/_4$in)

5mm ($^3/_{16}$in)

Ø 76mm (3in)

3mm ($^1/_8$in)

Ø 40mm (1$^9/_{16}$in) 2mm ($^5/_{64}$in)

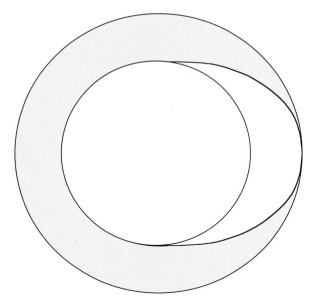

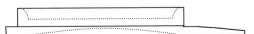

Box 43 | Jockey cap box   137

Box 44

Acorn box

She-oak and boxwood

l. 74mm (2²⁹/₃₂ in), d. 53mm (2³/₃₂ in)

There are probably hundreds of different varieties of oak trees in the world, and all will bear fruit in an acorn shape. Even so, there is no reason why the shape should not be manipulated, or modified, to suit your purpose. This particular box was modelled on an acorn I saw in America; as you see, it has a much wider cup than the English or common oak, but maybe I have exaggerated it still more than the original. It really does not matter – it is a box in the general shape of an acorn.

When mixing two different woods in a project, it is quite important to have them both at the same level of dryness. The easiest way to achieve this is to leave the final fitting of lid to base for a few days, or even weeks, after the rest of the work has been done. If they are not equally dry, there will be different amounts of movement in the two species as they stabilize in their new environment, and the fit of the lid will be compromised.

There is nothing in the making of this box that is not covered in other projects; however, I have seen other acorn boxes where the cup has been textured using an engineer's knurling tool to give a more effective finish.

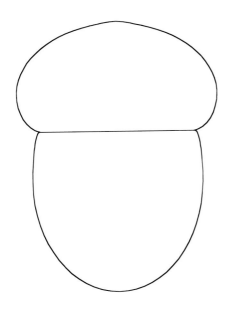

Acorn box

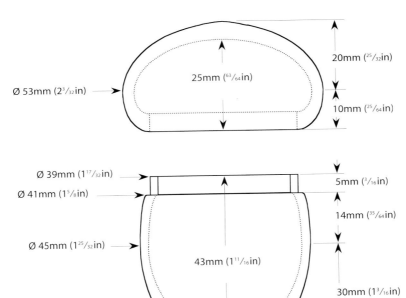

Ø 53mm (2³/₃₂ in)

25mm (⁶³/₆₄ in)

20mm (²⁵/₃₂ in)

10mm (²⁵/₆₄ in)

Ø 39mm (1¹⁷/₃₂ in)

Ø 41mm (1⁵/₈ in)

Ø 45mm (1²⁵/₃₂ in)

43mm (1¹¹/₁₆ in)

5mm (³/₁₆ in)

14mm (³⁵/₆₄ in)

30mm (1³/₁₆ in)

Box 44 | Acorn box   139

Box 45

Picture-frame insert box

Imbuya and maple burr

h. 52.5mm (2¹⁄₁₆in), d. 86mm (3²⁵⁄₆₄in)

The picture-frame technique is one that I particularly like to use, and I know of no other turner who uses it. It retains the original colour of the insert on the inside of the box, even when the outside has discoloured with age. This can be quite a significant difference with some woods, such as Osage orange, which is a vibrant yellow when fresh, but mellows to a dark tan quite quickly on exposure to bright light.

This technique also allows me to use small pieces of very special or rare woods without throwing most of it onto the floor as shavings. They can be cut into 6mm (¹⁄₄in) slices and glued to a supporting block to minimize wastage.

The box is started by holding what will be the base in the chuck. Then the top surface is cut to create the curved chamfer on the lid. This is the 'frame' for the insert. The next step is to drill down into the centre of the box, and widen the hole, leaving enough for the small ledge that holds the insert. This recess is cut with the 6mm (¹⁄₄in) square scraper, and the portion for the lid parted off from the base.

With the maple burr for the insert in the chuck, the outer surface can be cut, sanded and sealed, but not waxed. This will become the *inner* surface of the insert. It is then reduced in diameter until it just fits the recess in the lid. A sliding fit is better than a very tight one, as it gives more time to manoeuvre the lid onto the insert once the superglue has been applied. Accelerator is applied to the inner face whilst the lid is held in place. The inside of the lid can now be completed and, finally, the insert is parted off from its waste block.

The rest of the box follows previous patterns, except for the outer shape which in this case is made with a rounded bottom. Since this is a rocking box, I like to form a tiny hollow, 9.5mm (³⁄₈in) in diameter, in the centre of the base, which ensures that the box settles into a vertical position after rocking.

With burr wood there is no obvious grain direction, and the insert can be placed in any position. However, if I insert a piece that does have a definite grain, I always try to align it with the grain of the lid.

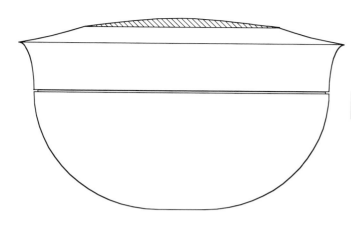

Picture-frame insert box

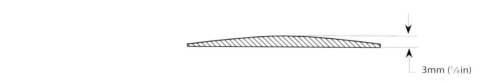

3mm (¹/₈in)

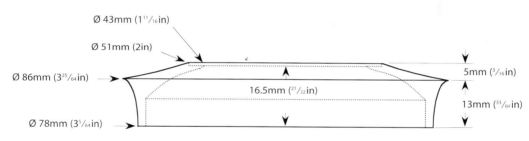

Ø 43mm (1¹¹/₁₆in)

Ø 51mm (2in)

Ø 86mm (3²⁵/₆₄in)

Ø 78mm (3⁵/₆₄in)

16.5mm (²¹/₃₂in)

5mm (³/₁₆in)

13mm (³³/₆₄in)

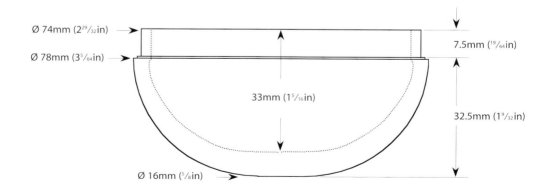

Ø 74mm (2²⁹/₃₂in)

Ø 78mm (3⁵/₆₄in)

7.5mm (¹⁹/₆₄in)

33mm (1⁵/₁₆in)

32.5mm (1⁹/₃₂in)

Ø 16mm (⁵/₈in)

Box 45 | Picture-frame insert box   141

Box 46

Three-centre spire box

Gonçalo alves

h. 186mm (7⁵/₁₆ in), max. d. 60mm (2³/₈ in)

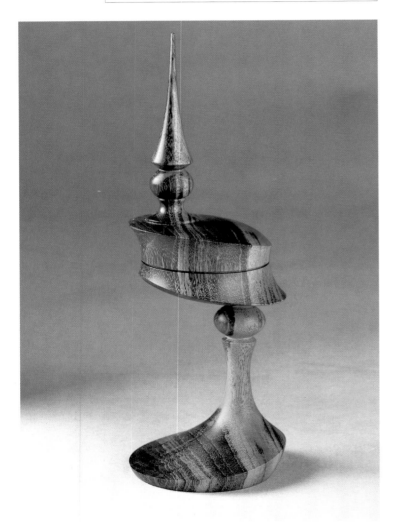

This project is easier to follow if the Commissionaire box (no. 40) has already been attempted.

It would have been easy to make this design in several pieces, but the challenge is to turn it in only two sections. The inside is completed in the normal manner, starting with the top, making sure that there is enough material for the off-centre finial on the lid, and the stem with its base on the lower part. The sides of the hollowed section are the only areas of the outside turned at this time. Remember to allow a reasonable thickness – about 6mm (¹/₄in) – at the top and bottom of the opening part to accommodate the off-centre cuts.

A piece of waste wood mounted on the eccentric chuck then needs to be cut to form a jam chuck for the top, as with the Commissionaire box. Once this is a very firm fit, the centre of the chuck can be moved. Obviously, the more it is moved over, the more eccentric, and effective, the box will be. Remember to align the grain with the reference marks and tape the lid to the jam chuck, as before.

It is a good idea to bring up the tailstock for support. A variable-speed lathe is a bonus, as the speed can be set low and increased slowly until a decent turning speed is achieved without vibration. Once the spire has been turned and the top finished, the jam chuck is returned to the original centre and cut to fit the body of the box. After moving the centre over, the stem can be turned, returning to the original centre to complete the base.

As long as small cuts are made, and each section is sanded and polished before moving the centre, a very distinctive box should be achieved.

A chuck in which the centre of the work can be moved to a new position parallel to the original is needed for this box. The basic idea was to make a staggered, extended, finial box, where the leg was offset in one direction and the spire in the other.

Three-centre spire box

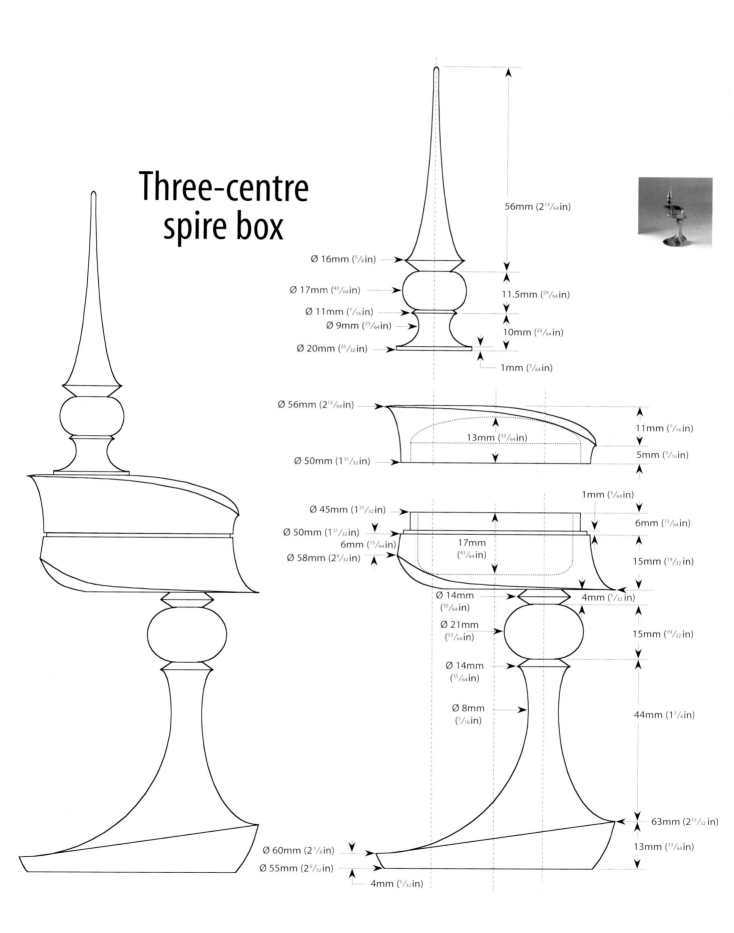

Ø 16mm ($^5/_8$in)

56mm ($2^{13}/_{64}$in)

Ø 17mm ($^{43}/_{64}$in)

11.5mm ($^{29}/_{64}$in)

Ø 11mm ($^7/_{16}$in)

Ø 9mm ($^{23}/_{64}$in)

10mm ($^{25}/_{64}$in)

Ø 20mm ($^{25}/_{32}$in)

1mm ($^3/_{64}$in)

Ø 56mm ($2^{13}/_{64}$in)

11mm ($^7/_{16}$in)

13mm ($^{33}/_{64}$in)

Ø 50mm ($1^{31}/_{32}$in)

5mm ($^3/_{16}$in)

1mm ($^3/_{64}$in)

Ø 45mm ($1^{25}/_{32}$in)

6mm ($^{15}/_{64}$in)

Ø 50mm ($1^{31}/_{32}$in)

17mm ($^{43}/_{64}$in)

6mm ($^{15}/_{64}$in)

15mm ($^{19}/_{32}$in)

Ø 58mm ($2^9/_{32}$in)

Ø 14mm ($^{35}/_{64}$in)

4mm ($^5/_{32}$in)

Ø 21mm ($^{53}/_{64}$in)

15mm ($^{19}/_{32}$in)

Ø 14mm ($^{35}/_{64}$in)

Ø 8mm ($^5/_{16}$in)

44mm ($1^3/_4$in)

63mm ($2^{15}/_{32}$in)

13mm ($^{33}/_{64}$in)

Ø 60mm ($2^3/_8$in)

Ø 55mm ($2^5/_{32}$in)

4mm ($^5/_{32}$in)

Box 46 | Three-centre spire box   143

Box 47

Lattice-lidded box
English boxwood
h. 25mm ($^{63}/_{64}$ in), d. 54mm ($2^1/_8$ in)

There are several turners demonstrating this type of decoration on boxes, but the one who has taken it to the highest level is Hans Weissflog. His designs are always more delicate and more intricate than any others I have seen.

The timber for a box of this design needs to be very close-grained and quite strong – hence my choice of boxwood. The shape of the box is not critical, except that it needs to have a flat top, so I kept the design very simple.

The procedure to be followed is much the same as with the Pill box (no. 13), with the following exceptions. Following the turning of the inside of the lid, the concentric rings are cut to a depth of 1.5mm ($^1/_{16}$ in). I tried using a tool ground from a masonry nail, and another attempt was made with a modified small screwdriver. However, I achieved a higher success rate with one of my Superthin parting tools, reground to give a small spike at the point. With this area sanded and polished, the rest of the inside of the box is completed.

The thickness of the top is obviously critical, so, after careful measuring, the lid is jam-chucked onto a spigot, mounted on the off-centre chuck, and the top surface cut flat, with rounded corners. To create an effective lattice, the amount of offset required is quite small; in this case the centre was moved about 10mm ($^3/_8$ in). When cutting the corners off the rings, in order to round them, vibration may cause the rings to shatter. There are two ways to stop this: first by making the spigot fit the inside shape closely, thereby supporting the top surface, and secondly, by placing a small piece of foam under the lid to give support.

Quite a lot of hand-sanding is required to finish the rings and remove any hairy bits in between them. With a little more experimental work on the tool for cutting the rings, I feel that these could be made still more delicate and intricate.

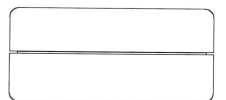

Lattice-lidded box

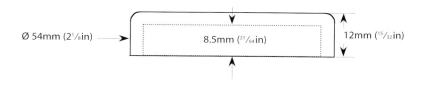

Ø 54mm (2¹/₈in) →   8.5mm (²¹/₆₄in)   12mm (¹⁵/₃₂in)

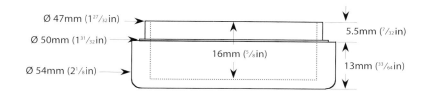

Ø 47mm (1²⁷/₃₂in) →   5.5mm (⁷/₃₂in)

Ø 50mm (1³¹/₃₂in) →   16mm (⁵/₈in)

Ø 54mm (2¹/₈in) →   13mm (³³/₆₄in)

Top of lid

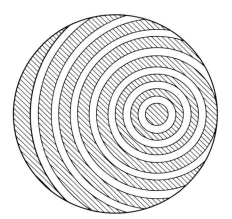

Underside of lid

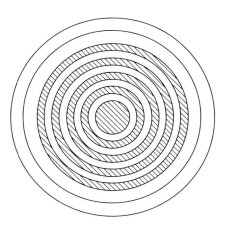

Box 47 | Lattice-lidded box   145

Box 48

Doughnut box

Putumuju

h. 40.5mm (1$^{19}/_{32}$ in), d. 73mm (2$^{7}/_{8}$ in)

The inspiration for this box should be obvious; however, having spent many happy days in America, I dedicate this box to the woodturners over there, who eat more doughnuts than any other people I know. This box is probably the most complex one in the book, because the lid fits on two spigots. Many students have problems getting a good fit on *one* spigot, so two should be a real test of accuracy.

The top is turned first, taking care to make sure that the inside faces are parallel, and square to the edge. The hole in the centre is cut from the inside, and the outer curve is completed with the top jam-chucked onto a scrap block.

To achieve a good fit on both spigots, a similar technique is used to the one described on pages 37–8 for inserting rings into the tops of boxes. An over-deep inner spigot is cut first to achieve a snug fit, then it is extended down into the base. After the outer spigot has been cut to size, the inner lip can be reduced to the depth of the outer spigot, to allow the faces to meet.

With the top in place, the hole and the outer curve are extended down into the base piece. With these areas defined, the lid is removed and the inner bottom recess cut. Finally the base is jam-chucked to complete the curve on the underside.

The only problem I encountered was that the recess in the base was too narrow for my finger, so it had to be sanded using abrasive held in some small forceps.

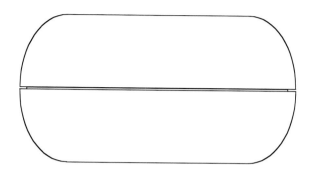

Doughnut box

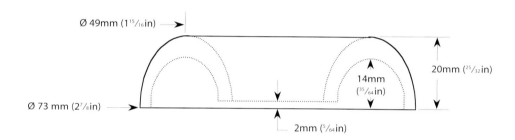

Ø 49mm (1¹⁵⁄₁₆ in)

20mm (²⁵⁄₃₂ in)

14mm (³⁵⁄₆₄ in)

Ø 73 mm (2⁷⁄₈ in)

2mm (⁵⁄₆₄ in)

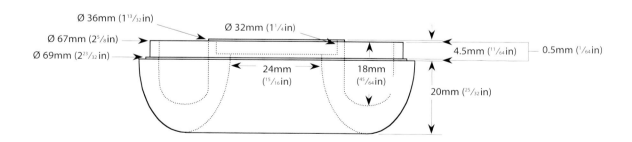

Ø 36mm (1¹³⁄₃₂ in)

Ø 32mm (1¹⁄₄ in)

Ø 67mm (2⁵⁄₈ in)

Ø 69mm (2²³⁄₃₂ in)

4.5mm (¹¹⁄₆₄ in)

0.5mm (¹⁄₆₄ in)

24mm (¹⁵⁄₁₆ in)

18mm (⁴⁵⁄₆₄ in)

20mm (²⁵⁄₃₂ in)

Box 48 | Doughnut box   147

Box 49

Off-centre oddity box

She-oak

h. 54mm (2⅛ in), d. 69mm (2²³/₃₂ in)

One notable feature of this design is that wherever two curved surfaces meet they create another, totally different curve. The box itself becomes almost secondary to the contrasting sculptural curves of the piece.

The inside of the box is created in the now normal manner, but must be kept quite small in relation to the overall size of the timber. The surfaces adjacent to the openings are cut in a curve to the edge of the timber. In order to allow jam-chucking on the Gim-Ball, a little preparation is needed. A no. 2 Morse taper is turned on a length of scrap wood, which is then fitted into the ball and secured with a wood screw. With the chuck set on the lathe centre line, a spigot needs to be cut to fit tightly on the inside of the box lid. The chuck is then slackened and the centre line pivoted, but only about 10–15°. After tightening the chuck, the top curve is cut in an ogee profile. Whilst the piece is spinning, a solid core can be seen surrounded by a blurred image. With a little practice it is possible to create a nice shape, although initially one is turning air most of the time.

Once you are satisfied with the top, the base can be turned in the same way.

As with all off-centre turning, it is essential to sand and polish at each stage before moving on to the next step.

This box requires a chuck in which the centre line can be pivoted, unlike the Three-Centre Spire box (no. 46), where the centres are parallel. However, the techniques needed to make it are basically the same. The only chuck I have capable of accomplishing this is the Multistar, fitted with the Gim-Ball accessory.

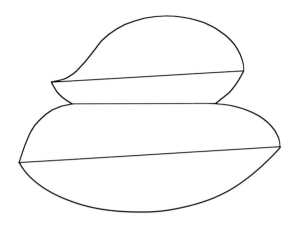

Off-centre oddity box

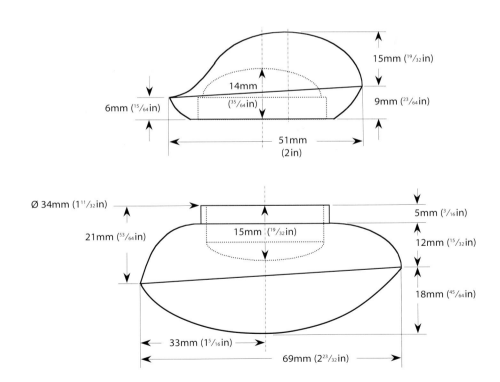

Box 49 | Off-centre oddity box 149

Box 50

Flask box

Osage orange and violet rosewood

h. 110mm (4¹¹/₃₂ in), d. 80mm (3⁵/₃₂ in)

An ancient, turned water flask was the inspiration for this box (see illustration opposite page 1). In recent years the technique has been revived and demonstrated by Johannes Rieber. I include it here as a project using multi-axis turning to achieve a very attractive item. It does, however, require a fair level of skill, and careful preparation.

Begin by preparing a piece of timber for the body, which needs to have the front and rear faces parallel. It must be a little longer than shown in the drawing to allow for trimming, and be nicely squared off at the ends. Mark the vertical centre line, and the centre points of the ends. Then mark the centre of the insert, and draw a circle of about 75mm (3in) diameter. You will find it helpful to mark the widths of the neck and base, as these lines will act as a guide during the cutting of the outer profile.

Mount the piece between centres with the four-point drive at the base, and drill the hole down the neck; this only needs to be about 25mm (1in) deep, just enough to penetrate the body of the flask. With the revolving centre riding in the hole, the outer profile needs to be cut using a spindle gouge. This may seem a little daunting at first, but the timber is balanced and can be rotated at quite a high speed. This makes the cutting easier, even though you are cutting air most of the time. When the shape is to your satisfaction, turn the neck and base. In order to finish off the top and bottom, a spigot to fit the hole is required. With the neck end jammed onto this, and the revolving centre in the tailstock supporting the base, the two ends can be trimmed to size. Sand, seal and polish all the turned areas.

Now drill a hole at the centre point of the insert and mount the flask on your screw chuck.

Turn a spigot on the rear face to fit your chuck. Holding the project by this spigot, turn the curved front face, and cut the hole where the insert will eventually fit; this hole needs to be of a size that you can hold on your expanding jaws.

Working through this hole, the interior of the flask can now be hollowed. As the wall thickness decreases the rubbish will start to spin out through the hole drilled in the neck, so this is a good guide to wall thickness. The more material you remove, the lighter the finished piece will be. Don't forget to sand, and polish the front.

The piece is now turned over and gripped with the jaws of the chuck expanded in the hole. The rear face can then be completed, first by removing most of the chucking spigot, then cutting a curve to match the front. Sand and polish as before.

Select a piece of contrasting wood for the insert, decorate the front if required, and create a spigot to fit the hole. This can then be parted off and glued in, after polishing.

The stopper can be made from a matching piece, and decorated in a similar fashion. This is accomplished by turning the stem first, then jamming this into a hole to complete the top surface.

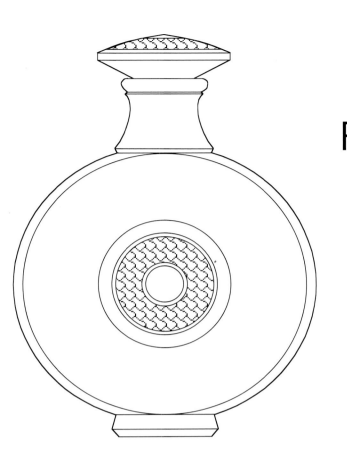

Flask box

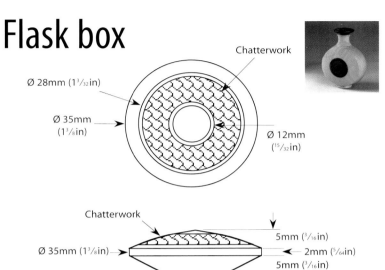

Chatterwork

Ø 28mm (1³/₃₂in)

Ø 35mm (1³/₈in)

Ø 12mm (¹⁵/₃₂in)

Chatterwork

Ø 35mm (1³/₈in)

Ø 16mm (⁵/₈in)

5mm (³/₁₆in)
2mm (⁵/₆₄in)
5mm (³/₁₆in)
10mm (²⁵/₆₄in)
4mm (⁵/₃₂in)

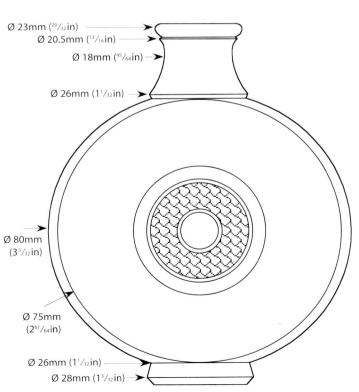

Ø 23mm (²⁹/₃₂in)
Ø 20.5mm (¹³/₁₆in)
Ø 18mm (⁴⁵/₆₄in)
Ø 26mm (1¹/₃₂in)
Ø 80mm (3⁵/₃₂in)
Ø 75mm (2⁶¹/₆₄in)
Ø 26mm (1¹/₃₂in)
Ø 28mm (1³/₃₂in)

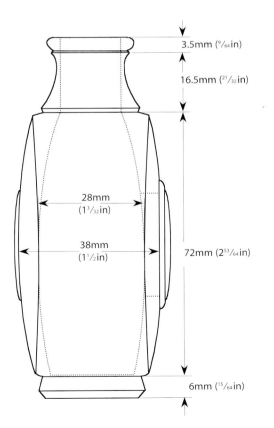

3.5mm (⁹/₆₄in)
16.5mm (²¹/₃₂in)
28mm (1³/₃₂in)
38mm (1¹/₂in)
72mm (2⁵³/₆₄in)
6mm (¹⁵/₆₄in)

Box 50 | Flask box 151

Part III
A Gallery
of Turned Boxes

Allan Batty

Allan was one of the first professional woodturners I met, at the first London *Practical Woodworking* show. He gave me the encouragement I needed to carry on and develop. Since then I have always valued his friendship, and appreciated the attention to detail that shows in his work.

Allan is what I would call one of the 'old school' of turners. He will happily turn staircase spindles and follow up with an intricate threaded box in alternative ivory. He started turning wood during his apprenticeship and has developed a reputation to be proud of.

The Secret Ball box pictured here is a marvel of precision engineering, and yet is produced on an ordinary lathe. The Nut and Bolt box shows his expertise in turning threads using only hand chasers.

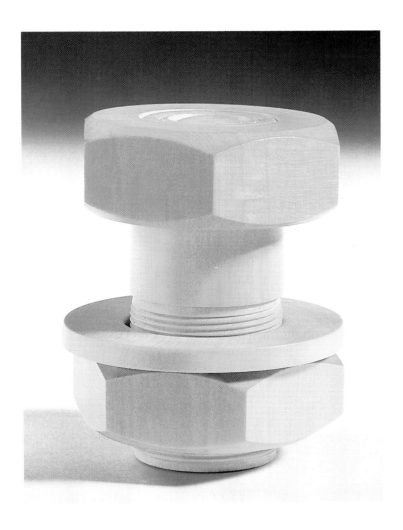

Allan Batty

This page and opposite:
Nut and Bolt secret box in boxwood

This page and opposite:
Secret Ball box in alternative ivory on pink ivory stand

Allan Batty

Allan Batty

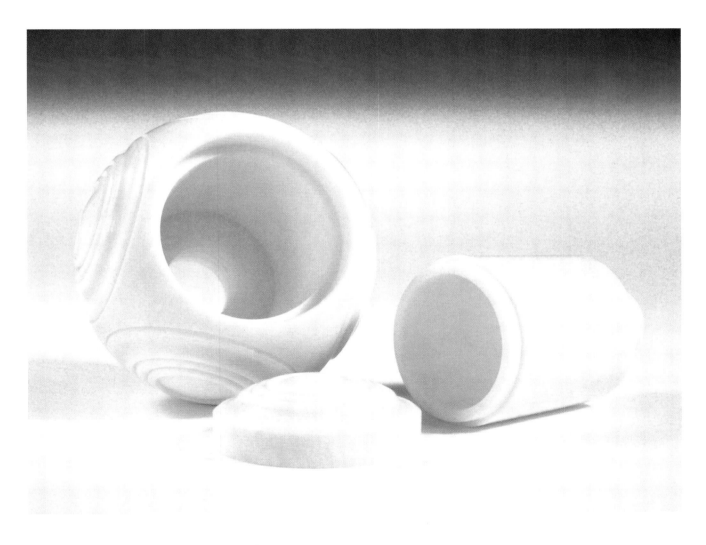

Kip Christensen

Kip is Professor of Technology Education and Co-ordinator of the Woodworking Technology Program at Brigham Young University, Provo, Utah. He is probably best known for his lidded containers, especially the ones made from elk and moose antler; however, all his work shows a feeling for design and balance, coupled with fine lines and attention to detail.

This page and opposite: **Lidded jewellery
container in elk antler, ebony and turquoise
h. 44mm (1³/₄ in), d. 92mm (3⁵/₈ in)**

Kip Christensen

Inlaid box in bird's-eye maple, African blackwood, pink ivory and turquoise
h. 63.5mm (2½ in), d. 89mm (3½ in)

Kip Christensen

Lidded box in ebony, cow bone, pink ivory and elk antler
h. 102mm (4in), d. 44mm (1¾in)

Michael Hosaluk

Michael is internationally recognized as one of the world's most creative woodturners. His ability to challenge the basic concept of a turned article, by cutting, carving and texturing, provides inspiration for anyone who wishes to break away from the basic round form that is achieved on the lathe.

Couples in ebonized maple
254 x 254 x 152mm (10 x 10 x 6in), oval cross section

Michael Hosaluk

Family in textured, burned and bleached maple
508 x 406 x 203mm (20 x 16 x 8in), oval cross section

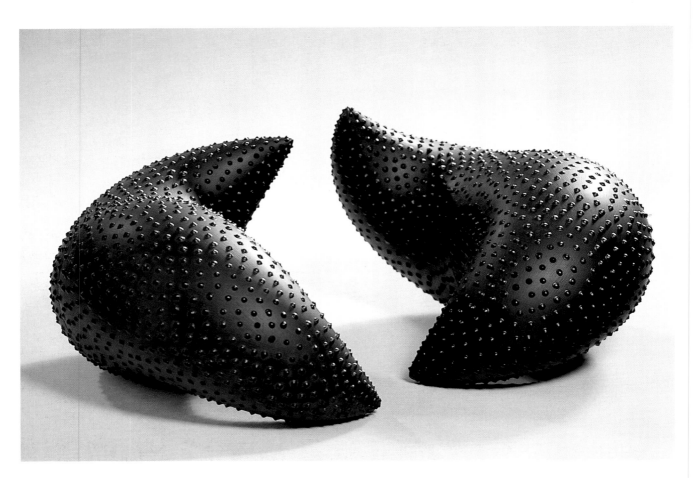

Michael Hosaluk

Couples in ebonized maple and acrylic gel
254 x 254 x 152mm (10 x 10 x 6in)

Family **in textured, burned and bleached maple**
508 x 406 x 203mm (20 x 16 x 8in), oval cross section

Ray Key

Ray was a well-respected international demonstrator before I had even thought of woodturning as a hobby. He has published three books on the subject, and made three videos; his dedication to woodturning is total. Ray was instrumental in forming the Association of Woodturners of Great Britain, and is now a life member and Honorary President. His work shows a clarity of line and form that is impossible to fault.

Cone boxes in African blackwood and pink ivory with stone cabochons

Left to right: **Soft round box in African blackwood with Masur birch insert, six-piece pagoda in African blackwood, round knobbed box in African blackwood with boxwood and pink ivory inserts**

Ray Key

Left to right: **Capsule box in burr boxwood with pink ivory insert, bowler hat box in Masur birch, four-piece pagoda in spalted beech**

Set of pagoda boxes in African blackwood: two-piece, three-piece, four-piece, five-piece, six-piece

Ray Key

Hans Joachim Weissflog

I have known Hans for a number of years, and his work still fascinates me. The boxes he creates on a normal lathe are truly amazing. His attention to detail, and the staggering variety of shapes he devises, make him the most innovative maker of turned boxes in the world today. Not so much a turner, more of a magician, is the way I think of him.

**Double-walled ball boxes in blackwood and boxwood
d. 80 and 50mm (3⁵/₃₂ and 1³¹/₃₂ in)**

A variety of intricate boxes
average d. about 50mm (2in)

Hans Joachim Weissflog

Hans Joachim Weissflog

This page and opposite: **Boxes using a wide range of materials
average d. about 50mm (2in)**

Metric conversion chart

Inches to millimetres

in	mm	in	mm	in	mm	in	mm
$\frac{1}{64}$	0.3969	$\frac{41}{64}$	16.2719	$1\frac{17}{32}$	38.8938	$2\frac{25}{32}$	70.6439
$\frac{1}{32}$	0.7937	$\frac{21}{32}$	16.6687	$1\frac{9}{16}$	39.6876	$2\frac{13}{16}$	71.4376
$\frac{3}{64}$	1.1906	$\frac{43}{64}$	17.0656	$1\frac{19}{32}$	40.4813	$2\frac{27}{32}$	72.2314
$\frac{1}{16}$	1.5875	$\frac{11}{16}$	17.4625	$1\frac{5}{8}$	41.2751	$2\frac{7}{8}$	73.0251
$\frac{5}{64}$	1.9844	$\frac{45}{64}$	17.8594	$1\frac{21}{32}$	42.0688	$2\frac{29}{32}$	73.8189
$\frac{3}{32}$	2.3812	$\frac{23}{32}$	18.2562	$1\frac{11}{16}$	42.8626	$2\frac{15}{16}$	74.6126
$\frac{7}{64}$	2.7781	$\frac{47}{64}$	18.6531	$1\frac{23}{32}$	43.6563	$2\frac{31}{32}$	75.4064
$\frac{1}{8}$	3.1750	$\frac{3}{4}$	19.0500	$1\frac{3}{4}$	44.4501	3	76.2002
$\frac{9}{64}$	3.5719	$\frac{49}{64}$	19.4469	$1\frac{25}{32}$	45.2438	$3\frac{1}{32}$	76.9939
$\frac{5}{32}$	3.9687	$\frac{25}{32}$	19.8437	$1\frac{13}{16}$	46.0376	$3\frac{1}{16}$	77.7877
$\frac{11}{64}$	4.3656	$\frac{51}{64}$	20.2406	$1\frac{27}{32}$	46.8313	$3\frac{3}{32}$	78.5814
$\frac{3}{16}$	4.7625	$\frac{13}{16}$	20.6375	$1\frac{7}{8}$	47.6251	$3\frac{1}{8}$	79.3752
$\frac{13}{64}$	5.1594	$\frac{53}{64}$	21.0344	$1\frac{29}{32}$	48.4188	$3\frac{5}{32}$	80.1689
$\frac{7}{32}$	5.5562	$\frac{27}{32}$	21.4312	$1\frac{15}{16}$	49.2126	$3\frac{3}{16}$	80.9627
$\frac{15}{64}$	5.9531	$\frac{55}{64}$	21.8281	$1\frac{31}{32}$	50.0063	$3\frac{7}{32}$	81.7564
$\frac{1}{4}$	6.3500	$\frac{7}{8}$	22.2250	2	50.8001	$3\frac{1}{4}$	82.5502
$\frac{17}{64}$	6.7469	$\frac{57}{64}$	22.6219	$2\frac{1}{32}$	51.5939	$3\frac{9}{32}$	83.3439
$\frac{9}{32}$	7.1437	$\frac{29}{32}$	23.0187	$2\frac{1}{16}$	52.3876	$3\frac{5}{16}$	84.1377
$\frac{19}{64}$	7.5406	$\frac{59}{64}$	23.4156	$2\frac{3}{32}$	53.1814	$3\frac{11}{32}$	84.9314
$\frac{5}{16}$	7.9375	$\frac{15}{16}$	23.8125	$2\frac{1}{8}$	53.9751	$3\frac{3}{8}$	85.7252
$\frac{21}{64}$	8.3344	$\frac{61}{64}$	24.2094	$2\frac{5}{32}$	54.7688	$3\frac{13}{32}$	86.5189
$\frac{11}{32}$	8.7312	$\frac{31}{32}$	24.6062	$2\frac{3}{16}$	55.5626	$3\frac{7}{16}$	87.3127
$\frac{23}{64}$	9.1281	$\frac{63}{64}$	25.0031	$2\frac{7}{32}$	56.3564	$3\frac{15}{32}$	88.1064
$\frac{3}{8}$	9.5250	1	25.4001	$2\frac{1}{4}$	57.1501	$3\frac{1}{2}$	88.9002
$\frac{25}{64}$	9.9219	$1\frac{1}{32}$	26.1938	$2\frac{9}{32}$	57.9439	$3\frac{17}{32}$	89.6939
$\frac{13}{32}$	10.3187	$1\frac{1}{16}$	26.9876	$2\frac{5}{16}$	58.7376	$3\frac{9}{16}$	90.4877
$\frac{27}{64}$	10.7156	$1\frac{3}{32}$	27.7813	$2\frac{11}{32}$	59.5314	$3\frac{19}{32}$	91.2814
$\frac{7}{16}$	11.1125	$1\frac{1}{8}$	28.5751	$2\frac{3}{8}$	60.3251	$3\frac{5}{8}$	92.0752
$\frac{29}{64}$	11.5094	$1\frac{5}{32}$	29.3688	$2\frac{13}{32}$	61.1189	$3\frac{21}{32}$	92.8689
$\frac{15}{32}$	11.9062	$1\frac{3}{16}$	30.1626	$2\frac{7}{16}$	61.9126	$3\frac{11}{16}$	93.6627
$\frac{31}{64}$	12.3031	$1\frac{7}{32}$	30.9563	$2\frac{15}{32}$	62.7064	$3\frac{23}{32}$	94.4564
$\frac{1}{2}$	12.7000	$1\frac{1}{4}$	31.7501	$2\frac{1}{2}$	63.5001	$3\frac{3}{4}$	95.2502
$\frac{33}{64}$	13.0969	$1\frac{9}{32}$	32.5438	$2\frac{17}{32}$	64.2939	$3\frac{25}{32}$	96.0439
$\frac{17}{32}$	13.4937	$1\frac{5}{16}$	33.3376	$2\frac{9}{16}$	65.0876	$3\frac{13}{16}$	96.8377
$\frac{35}{64}$	13.8906	$1\frac{11}{32}$	34.1313	$2\frac{19}{32}$	65.8814	$3\frac{27}{32}$	97.6314
$\frac{9}{16}$	14.2875	$1\frac{3}{8}$	34.9251	$2\frac{5}{8}$	66.6751	$3\frac{7}{8}$	98.4252
$\frac{37}{64}$	14.6844	$1\frac{13}{32}$	35.7188	$2\frac{21}{32}$	67.4689	$3\frac{29}{32}$	99.2189
$\frac{19}{32}$	15.0812	$1\frac{7}{16}$	36.5126	$2\frac{11}{16}$	68.2626	$3\frac{15}{16}$	100.013
$\frac{39}{64}$	15.4781	$1\frac{15}{32}$	37.3063	$2\frac{23}{32}$	69.0564	$3\frac{31}{32}$	100.806
$\frac{5}{8}$	15.8750	$1\frac{1}{2}$	38.1001	$2\frac{3}{4}$	69.8501	4	101.500

About the author

Born in Leeds, England, in 1939, Chris Stott became a professional woodturner in 1982. For about ten years he made his living by selling his work at craft fairs and shows, helped by his wife Cathy. Teaching and demonstrating then took over as the major part of his work. His first video, *A Lesson with Chris Stott: Turning Boxes* (1992), was an almost instant success. Since then he has produced eight more in the series, and another for the tool manufacturer Robert Sorby Ltd. He is also a regular contributor to *Woodturning* and other leading magazines.

As an invited demonstrator, Chris has participated in many international woodturning seminars in England, Ireland, Sweden, Germany and the USA. In 2001 he was invited to teach an intermediate-level course at Craft Supplies USA. He has travelled to Guernsey in the Channel Islands, Iceland, France and Norway, and gives regular demonstrations throughout England.

For many years he was a tutor at Craft Supplies (UK), and taught regularly at adult education centres. He was for several years the official demonstrator and one of the woodturning judges for the *Woodworker* shows at Alexandra Palace and Sandown Park. He also gave classes for Poolewood Machinery.

Chris is a member of the Association of Woodturners of Great Britain and the American Association of Woodturners, and is on the Register of Professional Turners with the Worshipful Company of Turners.

His work has been featured in a number of prestigious exhibitions, including Bonhams' *Decorative Arts Today* and *A Celebration of Craftsmanship* at Cheltenham, England. Some of his pieces are displayed at the Dansel Gallery in Abbotsbury, Dorset, and his work is represented in many private collections.

Rather than making large numbers of pieces, he prefers to concentrate on the design aspect of his work, experimenting with new techniques, especially involving the use of colour and texture to emphasize the grain patterns in the wood.

The video series *A Lesson with Chris Stott* comprises: *Turning Boxes, Turning Bowls, Cutting & Sharpening for Woodturners, Natural Edges & Hollow Forms, Decorative Effects & Colouring, First Steps in Woodturning, Finishing for Woodturners, Inlaid & Novelty Boxes* and *Basic Off-Centre Turning*.

Index

TITLES AVAILABLE FROM
GMC Publications
BOOKS

WOODCARVING

Beginning Woodcarving	GMC Publications
Carving Architectural Detail in Wood: The Classical Tradition	Frederick Wilbur
Carving Birds & Beasts	GMC Publications
Carving the Human Figure: Studies in Wood and Stone	Dick Onians
Carving Nature: Wildlife Studies in Wood	Frank Fox-Wilson
Carving on Turning	Chris Pye
Celtic Carved Lovespoons: 30 Patterns	Sharon Littley & Clive Griffin
Decorative Woodcarving (New Edition)	Jeremy Williams
Elements of Woodcarving	Chris Pye
Essential Woodcarving Techniques	Dick Onians
Lettercarving in Wood: A Practical Course	Chris Pye
Relief Carving in Wood: A Practical Introduction	Chris Pye
Woodcarving for Beginners	GMC Publications
Woodcarving Tools, Materials & Equipment (New Edition in 2 vols.)	Chris Pye

WOODTURNING

Bowl Turning Techniques Masterclass	Tony Boase
Chris Child's Projects for Woodturners	Chris Child
Contemporary Turned Wood: New Perspectives in a Rich Tradition	Ray Leier, Jan Peters & Kevin Wallace
Decorating Turned Wood: The Maker's Eye	Liz & Michael O'Donnell
Green Woodwork	Mike Abbott
Intermediate Woodturning Projects	GMC Publications
Keith Rowley's Woodturning Projects	Keith Rowley
Making Screw Threads in Wood	Fred Holder
Turned Boxes: 50 Designs	Chris Stott
Turning Green Wood	Michael O'Donnell
Turning Pens and Pencils	Kip Christensen & Rex Burningham
Woodturning: A Foundation Course (New Edition)	Keith Rowley
Woodturning: A Fresh Approach	Robert Chapman
Woodturning: An Individual Approach	Dave Regester
Woodturning: A Source Book of Shapes	John Hunnex
Woodturning Masterclass	Tony Boase
Woodturning Techniques	GMC Publications

WOODWORKING

Beginning Picture Marquetry	Lawrence Threadgold
Celtic Carved Lovespoons: 30 Patterns	Sharon Littley & Clive Griffin
Celtic Woodcraft	Glenda Bennett
Complete Woodfinishing (Revised Edition)	Ian Hosker
David Charlesworth's Furniture-Making Techniques	David Charlesworth
David Charlesworth's Furniture-Making Techniques – Volume 2	David Charlesworth
Furniture-Making Projects for the Wood Craftsman	GMC Publications
Furniture-Making Techniques for the Wood Craftsman	GMC Publications
Furniture Projects with the Router	Kevin Ley
Furniture Restoration (Practical Crafts)	Kevin Jan Bonner
Furniture Restoration: A Professional at Work	John Lloyd

Furniture Restoration and Repair for Beginners	Kevin Jan Bonner
Furniture Restoration Workshop	Kevin Jan Bonner
Green Woodwork	Mike Abbott
Intarsia: 30 Patterns for the Scrollsaw	John Everett
Kevin Ley's Furniture Projects	Kevin Ley
Making Chairs and Tables – Volume 2	GMC Publications
Making Classic English Furniture	Paul Richardson
Making Heirloom Boxes	Peter Lloyd
Making Screw Threads in Wood	Fred Holder
Making Woodwork Aids and Devices	Robert Wearing
Mastering the Router	Ron Fox
Pine Furniture Projects for the Home	Dave Mackenzie
Router Magic: Jigs, Fixtures and Tricks to Unleash your Router's Full Potential	Bill Hylton
Router Projects for the Home	GMC Publications
Router Tips & Techniques	Robert Wearing
Routing: A Workshop Handbook	Anthony Bailey
Routing for Beginners	Anthony Bailey
Sharpening: The Complete Guide	Jim Kingshott
Space-Saving Furniture Projects	Dave Mackenzie
Stickmaking: A Complete Course	Andrew Jones & Clive George
Stickmaking Handbook	Andrew Jones & Clive George
Storage Projects for the Router	GMC Publications
Veneering: A Complete Course	Ian Hosker
Veneering Handbook	Ian Hosker
Woodworking Techniques and Projects	Anthony Bailey
Woodworking with the Router: Professional Router Techniques any Woodworker can Use	Bill Hylton & Fred Matlack

UPHOLSTERY

Upholstery: A Complete Course (Revised Edition)	David James
Upholstery Restoration	David James
Upholstery Techniques & Projects	David James
Upholstery Tips and Hints	David James

TOYMAKING

Scrollsaw Toy Projects	Ivor Carlyle
Scrollsaw Toys for All Ages	Ivor Carlyle

DOLLS' HOUSES AND MINIATURES

1/12 Scale Character Figures for the Dolls' House	James Carrington
Americana in 1/12 Scale: 50 Authentic Projects	Joanne Ogreenc & Mary Lou Santovec
The Authentic Georgian Dolls' House	Brian Long
A Beginners' Guide to the Dolls' House Hobby	Jean Nisbett
Celtic, Medieval and Tudor Wall Hangings in 1/12 Scale Needlepoint	Sandra Whitehead
Creating Decorative Fabrics: Projects in 1/12 Scale	Janet Storey

CRAFTS

GARDENING

PHOTOGRAPHY

ART TECHNIQUES

VIDEOS

MAGAZINES

WOODTURNING ◆ WOODCARVING ◆ FURNITURE & CABINETMAKING
THE ROUTER ◆ NEW WOODWORKING ◆ THE DOLLS' HOUSE MAGAZINE
OUTDOOR PHOTOGRAPHY ◆ BLACK & WHITE PHOTOGRAPHY
TRAVEL PHOTOGRAPHY ◆ MACHINE KNITTING NEWS
GUILD OF MASTER CRAFTSMEN NEWS

The above represents a full list of all titles currently published or scheduled to be published.
All are available direct from the Publishers or through bookshops, newsagents and specialist retailers.
To place an order, or to obtain a complete catalogue, contact:

GMC Publications,
166 High Street Lewes East Sussex BN7 1XU United Kingdom
Tel: 01273 488005 Fax: 01273 402866
E-mail: pubs@thegmcgroup.com

Orders by credit card are accepted